Cabinet Making for Beginners

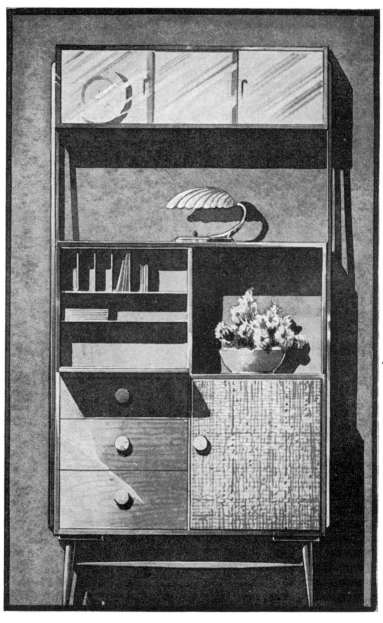

ROOM DIVIDER OR WALL CABINET WITH GOOD ACCOMMODATION
The door is covered with weave-pattern plastic material
Length 3 ft., height 6 ft., depth 1 ft. 6 ins.

Cabinet Making for Beginners

Tools, Joints, Cabinet Construction,
Veneering and Inlaying, Drawing,
Cutting Lists, etc., Timber, Fittings,
Typical Designs

Charles H. Hayward

Drake Publishers Inc.
381 Park Avenue South
New York, N.Y. 10016

VERSO

ISBN 87749-064-3

L.C.C.C.N. 78-24432

Published in 1971 by
Drake Publishers Inc.
381 Park Avenue South
New York, N.Y. 10016

Second Printing 1972

© Charles H. Hayward 1971

Printed in New York U.S.A.

CONTENTS

INTRODUCTION

ALTHOUGH basically the working of wood by hand has not changed for a couple of centuries or more, there have in recent years been introduced several new materials which have necessitated a considerable revision of methods of construction so far as modern design in furniture is concerned. We refer, of course, to the availability of really reliable plywood, laminated board, chipboard, and hardboard which have made possible the use of wide, flat surfaces without any of the drawbacks (in particular that of shrinkage) that attend the use of solid wood. Circumstances too have had their effect. For instance, the shortage of timber has resulted in the almost complete disappearance of many hardwoods in solid form, with the result that veneering has become a necessity rather than an alternative way of producing a certain result. Another point is the growth of the machine even in the " hand " shop. Few craftsmen to-day, even the most rigid of the old school, would think of ripping timber from the rough, or of thicknessing it; and many of them have installed mortising machines, and even a router. This is a development which has to be reckoned with in any book on cabinet work, because, even though a man's training is in hand work, he needs to know just what the capabilities (and limitations) of a machine are. In any case most timber is bought ready-sawn into boards, and is frequently thicknessed, so that any man buying such timber may be reckoned to be using machinery to that extent.

In the following pages we have dealt with the modern methods of construction and have also included the more conventional systems which belong to solid wood and which experience has shown to be sound. The handling of fundamental tools is explained since ability to use tools lies at the root of all workshop practice, and we have given notes on basic machines and the work they are capable of. Joints, too, and their application to this or that job are given a special chapter, with notes on those specially suitable for machine cutting, and drawing, marking out, and timbers are explained. Those seeking fuller information on any of these subjects should refer to the other volumes in this series: *Tools for Woodwork*, *Practical Veneering*, *Timbers for Woodwork*, *Woodwork Joints*, *Carpentry for Beginners*, *English Period Furniture*, *Garden Woodwork*, *Practical Wood Carving and Gilding*, *Practical Carpentry and Joinery*, *Making Toys in Wood*, *Staining and Polishing*, *Practical Upholstery*, *Junior Woodworker*, *The Practical Wood Turner*, and *Light Machines for Woodwork*.

CABINET MAKING
FOR BEGINNERS

CHAPTER I. THE KIT OF TOOLS

WHEN you set out to buy tools there is a golden rule to keep in mind ; buy the best you can afford. The reason why two tools of similar appearance should have widely differing prices may not be immediately apparent, but it will come out in the long run. Good, reliable tools cannot be produced below a certain figure, and if you pay less than this you will be storing up trouble for yourself in precise ratio to the money you may save now. The best plan is to go to a reliable tool merchant and cheerfully pay his catalogue prices.

You do not need a " complete kit " straightway (if there is any such thing), but there are certain fundamental tools which you must have to be able to make a start at all. The following list, although it does not represent all the tools which a cabinet maker needs for all branches of his craft, will enable you to do all the cabinet work you are likely to tackle. For simpler work, you will not need all of these, and those marked with an asterisk can be bought later as the necessity for them arises.

The question of machines necessarily arises. We are not thinking of the large type used in the modern mass-production shop which, once set up, are used to turn out huge quantities of parts all to a pattern, but rather of the light type which the small cabinet maker or the home craftsman might install to save time in the everyday jobs that constantly occur. Operations such as the ripping out of timber, edging, and thicknessing, and often mortising are seldom done by hand to-day.

One final word. Having paid a fair price, give your tools fair usage. Keep them in condition, and don't use them for work for which they were never intended.

Those seeking fuller information on tools and machines should see the companion volumes, *Tools for Woodwork*, and *Light Machines for Woodwork*.

THE TOOL KIT

Tools marked with an asterisk can follow as occasion requires.

Saws

CROSS-CUT SAW, 26 in., 8–9 points per inch.

*PANEL SAW, 20 in., 10–12 points per inch.

TENON SAW, 14 in., 14 points per inch.

DOVETAIL SAW, 8 in., 18–22 points per inch.

BOW SAW, 12 in.

*KEYHOLE SAW, about 11 in.

To avoid the expense of two backsaws, you can obtain one of 9–10 in., with about 16 points per inch. This will do for general bench work, dovetails, and small tenons, larger tenons being cut with the panel saw. It is better to have the two saws, however.

Planes

JACK PLANE, wood, $2\frac{1}{8}$-in. cutter.

SMOOTHING PLANE, metal, $2\frac{1}{4}$-in. or $2\frac{3}{8}$-in. cutter

TRYING PLANE, wood or metal, 22 in. long, $2\frac{3}{8}$-in. cutter.

*PANEL PLANE, metal, 15 in. long.

*TOOTHING PLANE, 2-in. cutter.

*BLOCK PLANE, $1\frac{1}{4}$-in. cutter.

*COMPASS PLANE, $1\frac{3}{4}$-in. cutter.

REBATE PLANE, wood or metal, 1-in. to $1\frac{1}{2}$-in. cutter.

*BULLNOSE PLANE, 1-in. cutter.

*SHOULDER PLANE, $1\frac{1}{4}$-in. cutter.

PLOUGH PLANE, metal or wood, $\frac{1}{8}$-in. to $\frac{1}{2}$-in. cutter.

*MOULDING PLANES. Obtain only as needed.

The choice of wood or metal planes is largely personal. The former cost less and in capable hands turn out perfectly good work. Metal planes are easier to use, are generally adjustable, and are preferable for some work.

Chisels and Gouges

FIRMER CHISELS, * $\frac{1}{8}$ in., $\frac{1}{4}$ in., $\frac{1}{2}$ in., 1 in.

BEVELLED-EDGE CHISELS, $\frac{3}{4}$ in., *$1\frac{1}{4}$ in.

SASH MORTISE CHISELS, *$\frac{1}{4}$ in., $\frac{5}{16}$ in., *$\frac{3}{8}$ in.

*OUTSIDE-GROUND GOUGES.

*INSIDE-GROUND GOUGES.

Obtain as required. Not used widely in cabinet work.

*DRAWER-LOCK CHISEL.

Brace and Bits

RATCHET BRACE, 8 in. to 10 in. sweep.

TWIST BITS, $\frac{1}{4}$in., $\frac{3}{8}$in., *$\frac{1}{2}$in., *$\frac{3}{4}$in.

*HALF-TWIST BIT, $\frac{1}{4}$ in.

*SHELL BITS, $\frac{1}{8}$ in., $\frac{3}{16}$ in.

DRILL BITS, $\frac{1}{8}$ in., $\frac{3}{16}$ in.

CENTRE BITS, *$\frac{1}{2}$ in., $\frac{3}{4}$ in., *1 in.

SNAIL COUNTERSINK, $\frac{1}{2}$ in.

*ROSE COUNTERSINK, $\frac{1}{2}$ in.

*TURNSCREW BIT.

*EXPANSION BIT.

BRADAWLS, about $\frac{3}{32}$in., and $\frac{1}{8}$ in.

Other Tools

WOOD SPOKESHAVE, 2¼ in.
*METAL SPOKESHAVE, 2 in.
(round-face).
ROUTER (wood or metal).
WOOD FILE, 7 in.
*WOOD RASP, 7 in.
SCRAPER, 5 in.
MARKING GAUGE.
CUTTING GAUGE.
MORTISE GAUGE.
TRY SQUARE, 6 in., and 12 in.
MITRE SQUARE, 12 in.
*SLIDING BEVEL, 9 in.
*LARGE TRY SQUARE, 30 in.
(home made).
HAMMER, Warrington, about
8 oz.
*HAMMER, pattern maker's,
about 3 oz.
MALLET, about 6 in.
PINCERS, 8 in.
SCREWDRIVERS, 8 in., 5 in.
(ratchet).

RULE, 2 ft. or 3 ft., folding.
OILSTONE, 8 in.
*OILSTONE SLIP, about 4 in.
by 1 in.
PUNCHES, medium and small
(hollow point).
*DIVIDERS, 6 in.
VENEERING HAMMER
(home made).
CORK RUBBER, about 4½ in.
*SCRATCH, about 7 in. (home
made).
MITRE BLOCK, 9 in. (home made).
*MITRE BOX, for 4-in. moulding
(home made).
*MITRE SHOOTING-BOARD, about
18 in. (home made).
*MITRE SHOOTING-BLOCK (home
made).
SHOOTING-BOARD, 2 ft. and
*5 ft. (home made).
BENCH HOOK (home made).
MITRE TEMPLATE (home made)

Cramps

SASH CRAMPS, metal, pair 24 in.,
pair *42 in.
HANDSCREWS, 8 in., one pair at
least, more when needed.
*G-CRAMPS, 8 in. to 10 in. work.
One pair, more when needed.

THUMBSCREWS, 2½ in. Half a
dozen at least.
*SPRING DOGS, 4 in., as required.
*SPRING CLOTHES PEGS, as
required.

Machines

CIRCULAR SAW, 9-in. saw minimum. Rise-and-fall and
tilting table or saw. Groove
for mitre gauge.
EDGER, 4–6 in. Preferably with
thicknessing attachment.
BAND SAW. Tilting table. 9–
12-in. wheels.

In some respects the bandsaw can be regarded as an
alternative to the circular saw,
but each is capable of certain
operations which the other cannot tackle. See further notes
on page 40.

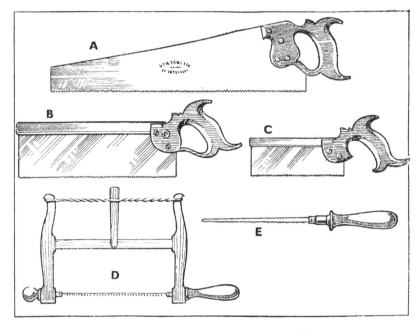

FIG. I. SAWS USED IN CABINET MAKING.

A. CROSS-CUT SAW.—For sawing across the grain (though it can be used equally well *with* the grain). Length 26 in. ; teeth 8–9 points per inch.

A. PANEL SAW.—Suitable for thin wood, tenons, and large joints. Size 20 in., with 10–12 points per inch.

B. TENON SAW.—Used for cutting tenons and general bench work. Length 14 in. ; teeth 14 points per inch.

C. DOVETAIL SAW.—For dovetailing and small work generally. Length 8 in. ; teeth 18–22 points per inch.

D. BOW SAW.—For cutting shapes. Length 12 in.

E. KEYHOLE SAW.—For internal shapes which the bow saw cannot reach. Blade length 11 in.

The sizes suggested above are founded on what experience has shown to be suitable for cabinet work. A little one way or the other will not make much difference. Do not attempt to sharpen your saws unless you have had experience. It will not prove an economy in the long run. If you do attempt it, make a start on the largest toothed saw you have.

A feature common to all saws is " set " ; that is, the teeth are bent outwards alternately at each side. This makes the saw kerf wider than the blade thickness so enabling the latter to clear easily without binding. In addition best modern handsaws are taper ground, the back being thinner than the toothed edge. This means that less set is needed for clearance, and as a consequence the saw cuts more rapidly because it has less sawdust to remove. The pitch or angle of the teeth varies with the saw. Saws for fine work have their teeth tilted well back as they are then less liable to tear out the grain. The filing angle or bevel, i.e., the angle the file makes with the blade when sharpening is 60 deg.

One last point is the size of teeth. The larger the tooth the faster the cut and the rougher the finish. Choice is a matter of compromise. Size is known as " points per inch ". Thus a saw having ten actual points in an inch including those at both ends would be a " 10 point " saw. As an actual example a " 9 point " saw would have exactly ⅛ in. between each of its points.

SAWS

There are three general kinds of saws you need : handsaws, A, Fig. 1, for the preliminary cutting out of timber ; backsaws, B and C, for bench work, cutting joints, and small work generally ; and saws for cutting shapes, D and E. So far as their use is concerned, the same general rules apply to all.

Firstly, don't force the saw in an effort to make it cut more quickly. It will probably result in the blade becoming buckled and may cause it to drift from the line. Little more power is needed than the effort of keeping the saw moving. A certain pressure is required, even if only for the necessity of exercising positive control, but if the saw is not cutting as quickly as it should it probably needs sharpening.

Secondly, start the cut properly. One of the chief causes of failure in sawing is due to the cut being started out of truth. The saw drifts from the line, and in an effort to correct it the blade is twisted, with

FIG. 2. USING THE CROSS-CUT SAW.
To start the cut let the blade bear against the thumb of the left hand. Pointing the index finger gives maximum control.

the result that it becomes permanently buckled. Remember that both handsaws and backsaws are intentionally put into a state of tension during their manufacture, and buckling a saw interferes with this with disastrous results.

If you wish to sharpen your own saws, make a start on one with large teeth. Dovetail saws are extremely difficult to sharpen, and the cost of putting right a saw which has been badly sharpened is more than what you may have saved in doing your own sharpening.

Handsaws

Cross - cutting. The most usual way of using the handsaw is with the wood supported upon trestles, or upon the bench. Fig. 2 shows the latter operation in which the worker is just starting to cross-cut a board. Note how the index finger points along the blade. This gives maximum control of the saw and is a rule applying to backsaws as well as handsaws. The left hand grips the far edge of the board and the thumb bears against the blade, whilst a few short strokes are made to get the saw started in the right position and direction.

FIG. 3. OVERHAND RIPPING ON BENCH.
Start the cut by pointing the saw forwards and upwards. When the kerf has been started assume the position shown here.

As soon as a reasonable start has been made the short strokes are changed for long, even ones, the thumb of the left hand still bearing against the saw blade until the saw has entered the wood about its own depth. The reason for keeping the thumb against the blade is a safety-first one. If the blade should jump out of its kerf the thumb prevents it from jagging across the knuckles. As a rule a handscrew is used to hold the wood still. When cutting on trestles the knee bears down on the wood to steady it. As the end of the cut is reached bring the left hand over the saw and support the over-hanging end.

Ripping. The procedure of ripping a board on the trestles is similar. It is necessary, however, to shift the board forward after a few inches have been sawn so as to clear the trestles. When a foot or so has been cut the board can be pulled back and the saw worked between

SAW CUTS ON WASTE SIDE

FIG. 4. POINT TO NOTE WHEN SAWING.
If the saw is taken directly on the line the resulting wood will be too small. Cut to one side as shown here.

the trestles. It is obviously important to hold the saw upright, and an excellent plan is to place a try square on the board near the saw. This will enable you to judge whether it is upright.

There is a second method of ripping frequently used by cabinet makers known as overhand ripping (see Fig. 3). To start the cut the saw is held at a slight upward angle at the near corner and a few strokes made. It is then held with both hands in the manner shown. The method is less back-breaking than the other, and

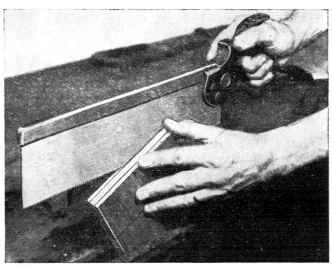

FIG. 5. FIRST STAGE WHEN SAWING A TENON.
Fix the wood in the vice at a slight angle and start the saw at the corner. In this way both top and near gauge lines can be seen. Reverse the wood, this time upright, and complete the cut.

enables you to judge better whether the saw is being held upright. Note that the work must be held down with handscrews.

We may note here a detail which applies to most sawing operations. When wood is marked out, whether it be with the gauge or pencil, it is invariably to the finished size. It is clear, then, that it would not do to saw right on the line because it would result in the work finishing too small. Instead, the saw is held on the *waste* side of the line so that the latter is just left in. This enables the work to be trimmed to the final size with the plane. Fig. 4 shows the idea.

Backsaws

The use of these two saws is identical, except that the tenon saw, B, Fig. 1, is used for large work, and the dovetail, C, for fine work.

It is just a case of exercising discretion as to which is the more suitable for any particular job.   Fig. 5 shows the first stage in cutting a tenon.   The wood is held at an angle so that both front and top edges can be seen.   This is a great help in sawing square.   When the saw has been taken down to approximately the diagonal the wood is reversed in the vice, this time upright, and the cut completed. The note previously given about holding the saw on the waste side of the line applies equally in the present instance.

Fig. 6 shows the use of the bench hook.   It is a device for steadying the wood, and consists of three pieces of wood screwed or dowelled

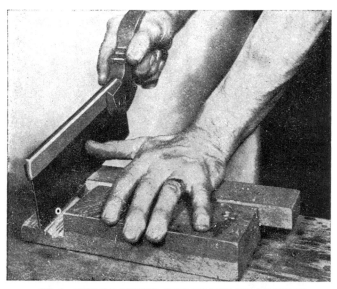

FIG. 6. USING DOVETAIL SAW ON THE BENCH HOOK.
Note how the saw bears against the left-hand thumb to steady it at the start of the cut. The ball of the left hand presses against the wood.

together.   Exact sizes are immaterial, the only point to note in making it being that the lower front piece which rests against the bench edge should be fixed with dowels.   Nails or screws must not be used because with continuous use the base becomes worn away, and the saw might be jarred across the metal.

Note from Fig. 6 how the thumb of the left hand bears against the blade when starting the cut, whilst the palm presses down and steadies the wood.   See also how the saw is started at the far corner and is tilted forwards slightly.   As the cut deepens the saw is gradually brought to a horizontal position. For a start it is wise always to square a line on both top and front edges as a guide, even when the cut is not an important one. It is necessary to get into the habit of sawing square as soon as possible.

Saws for Cutting Curves

Bow saw. The advantage of the bow saw, D, Fig. 1, is that, since the blade is held at both ends and is so kept in tension, there is no liability for it to become buckled. This means that the

FIG. 7. CUTTING SHAPE WITH BOW SAW, WOOD HELD IN VICE.
The wood should be kept as low as possible to prevent vibration. Square sawing is clearly important, the blade being kept horizontal as well as square laterally.

blade can be comparatively narrow and so able to negotiate quick curves. In fact, the only limitation to its use is bounded by the distance of the blade from the centre bar. It cannot cut at a greater distance than this from the edge. The fact that the blade can be turned to cut in any direction, however, enables long cuts to be made providing that the cut is near a side edge. Revolving the handles at the ends turns the blade, and it is obviously necessary to see that both are in alignment before beginning the cut. This is done by sighting the blade—that is by looking across it straight at the teeth ; any winding will be apparent.

Two hands are used to grasp the saw as shown in Fig. 7, and the

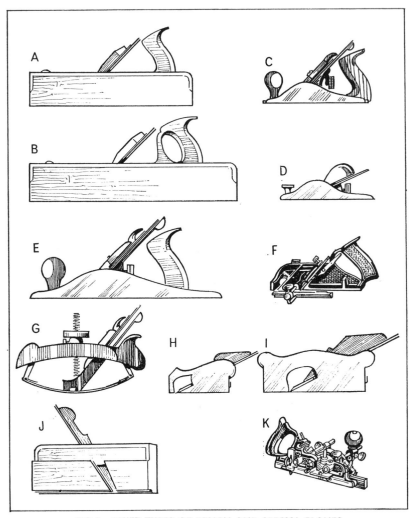

FIG. 8. CHIEF TYPES OF BENCH AND SPECIAL PLANES.

See opposite page.

important point is to keep it square in both directions. One soon acquires the knack of gradually turning the saw to follow the curve. The wood is held in the vice with as little projection as possible ; otherwise it is liable to chatter, and if it is somewhat thin it may even split. In the case of internal cuts the blade is disconnected from one of the handles by driving out the holding rivet. This enables it to be threaded through a hole previously bored in the wood. Twisting the cord at the top of the saw gives the tension to the blade. It should be released when the saw is finished with.

Keyhole saw. In the case of the keyhole saw, E, no tension is possible, of course. The tool has to rely upon the stiffness of the blade. It has to be fairly thick to resist the strain and it makes a coarse cut in consequence. Furthermore it has to widen considerably towards the base for the same reason. This in turn prevents it from cutting very acute curves. The rule is to give the blade as little projection as is consistent with a reasonable stroke. This minimises the tendency for the blade to buckle. Two hands are used for the saw.

Veneer saw. Although not a necessity this is handy for cutting thick veneer. It is curved at the cutting edge so that the corners do not dig in. It is worked up against a straight-edge.

PLANES

If there are many varieties of planes, remember that there are many different jobs to be done with the plane. Planes are needed to reduce the thickness of a piece of wood, straighten its edge, smooth its surface, trim joints, work a rebate, or form a groove. Some are of wood and the other of metal, but you will not need both. The choice is largely one of personal preference. A quite good plan is to have a wood jack plane and trying plane, and a smoothing and panel or fore plane of metal.

Bench Planes

The use and sharpening of planes is similar though they come in for somewhat different purposes. The jack plane is for the rougher sort of work such as removing saw marks, and the quick reduction of thickness, and is normally set fairly coarse. The trying plane,

A. JACK PLANE, WOOD.—For removing thick shavings and rough work.

B. TRYING PLANE, WOOD.—For planing joints and truing work. Length 22–24 in., cutter 2½ in.

C. SMOOTHING PLANE, IRON, ADJUSTABLE.—Cleaning up surfaces and general bench work. Length 10 in., cutter 2⅜ in.

D. BLOCK PLANE.—For trimming small work. 1¼ in.–1⅝ in. cutter.

E. PANEL PLANE, IRON, ADJUSTABLE.—Truing fairly small work and trimming. Length 15 in., cutter 2⅛ in.

E. FORE PLANE, IRON, ADJUSTABLE.—Length 18 in., cutter 2⅜ in.

F. REBATE AND FILLISTER PLANE, IRON.—For working rebates. Cutter 1½ in.

G. COMPASS PLANE.—For cleaning up circular shapes. 1¾ in. cutter.

H. BULLNOSE PLANE.—For working small rebates and other small work. Cutter 1 in.

I. SHOULDER PLANE.—For trimming large shoulders and fine rebates, especially end grain. 1¼ in. cutter.

J. MOULDING PLANE.—In various patterns according to moulding.

K. PLOUGH OR UNIVERSAL PLANE.—For working grooves and sometimes beads and reeds. Cutters range upwards from ⅛ in.

being long, is for truing surfaces and edges and must be set fine. The smoothing plane comes in for the final cleaning up of surfaces and again is set fine.

FIG. 9. PLANING AN EDGE WITH THE JACK PLANE.
The fingers of the left hand curl beneath the sole and touch the wood, so acting as a fence and keeping the plane from moving from side to side.

Trying plane. When using either the jack, A, Fig. 8, or the trying plane, B, on an edge, hold it as in Fig. 9. Notice specially that the fingers of the left hand curl down beneath the sole and touch the surface of the wood. In this way they act as a sort of fence and help in keeping the plane in alignment along the edge. When

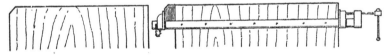

FIG. 10. CORNER CHISELLED OFF.   **FIG. II. BLOCK CRAMPED ON TO STOP SPLITTING.**
When end grain is being trimmed the far corner is liable to split. If the wood is wide enough the corner can be taken off. Otherwise the block shown in Fig. II must be cramped on and the corner of this chiselled.

beginning the stroke exert extra pressure with the left hand, and gradually transfer it to the right hand as the far end is reached. This prevents the ends from being dubbed over. If the edge is out of square don't try to rock the plane. Instead push the plane over to the side requiring a thicker shaving, because, the cutter being slightly rounded, this brings the part of the cutter with the greatest projection into action on the high part.

The treatment of end grain is similar except that precautions have to be taken to prevent the grain from splitting out at the far end. One plan when there is sufficient width of wood is to chisel off the corner as in Fig. 10. The alternative, Fig. 11, is used when the wood is not wide enough to permit chiselling.

Shooting-board. In the case of thin wood the plane would be liable to wobble when treating the edge, and the shooting board is used as in Fig. 12. The wood lies flat on the thick part of the board, and the plane is worked along the edge. Incidentally, it is invaluable for squaring the ends of timber. The wood is held fast

FIG. 12. PLANING AN EDGE ON THE SHOOTING-BOARD.
The edge of the wood overhangs so that the wood is made straight by the truth of the plane sole. For squaring an end, however, the plane must be kept up to the edge of the upper platform, and the wood held close up to the stop.

against the stop, and, since the latter is at right angles with the edge, the wood is bound to be planed square. For end grain the corner must either be chiselled off first, or a spare piece of wood parallel in its width must be held between the wood and the stop. When planing joints one piece is held face-side uppermost, and the other face-side downwards. This ensures the pieces being in alignment.

Smoothing plane. This is shown in use in Fig. 13. It should not be used until the surface has been trued up with the trying plane —unless the wood has already been machine planed.

In common with all metal planes, it needs a lubricant, and for this a wad of cotton wool soaked in linseed oil is excellent. Note

FIG. 13. CLEANING A JOINT USING IRON SMOOTHING PLANE.
When planing across the grain plane into an edge whenever possible as this helps to avoid splitting.

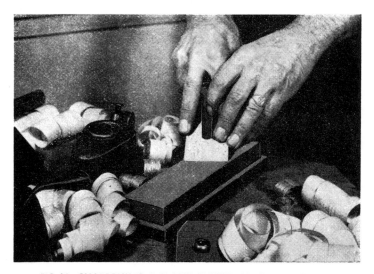

FIG. 14. SHARPENING A PLANE CUTTER ON THE OILSTONE.
Afterwards the cutter is reversed *flat* on the stone. To remove the burr the cutter is stropped on leather dressed with fine emery and oil, and finished finally by hand stropping.

how the plane is used at an angle in Fig. 13. This gives a slicing cut which is not so liable to tear out the cross-grain. Also, by having a bearing on the adjoining rail, it is more likely to keep flat.

Sharpening. When a plane is new the cutter is ground, but it needs to be sharpened on the oilstone. Remove the wedge by tapping with the hammer the front of the jack or trying plane. In the case of the wood smoothing plane the back is tapped. Metal planes have either a lever cap which is raised, or a screw which is undone. Loosen the bolt which holds the back iron, and pour a few drops of oil on to the stone.

Place the cutter on the stone with the bevel lying flat, and raise the hands *slightly* so that just the edge is touching. Work it back and forth as in Fig. 14 until a burr is turned up at the back. This can be detected by drawing the thumb *across* the edge at the back. Now reverse the cutter *flat* on the stone and rub it once or twice. This is to loosen the burr. At all costs avoid dubbing over the edge. To remove the burr draw the edge across the corner of

FIG. 15. SIGHTING THE PLANE WHEN SETTING.

In a metal plane all adjustment is by screw or lever. In a wood plane either the cutter or the striking knob are tapped with the hammer.

a piece of wood, and strop the edge on a piece of leather. A keen edge cannot be seen. A dull one shows up as a thin line of light.

Setting. Replace the back iron, adjusting it in accordance with the work the plane has to do. Its purpose is to break the shaving as it is raised and so minimise any tendency of the grain to tear out. The closer to the edge it is set the more effective it becomes, but the greater the resistance it offers. It is, therefore, a matter of compromise. For the jack plane it can be set about $\frac{1}{16}$ in. from the edge ; the trying plane (when set fine) about $\frac{1}{32}$ in., the smoothing plane $\frac{1}{32}$ in., or less.

Fig. 15 shows how the plane is set. A piece of paper on the bench enables the cutter to be sighted. It should appear as a thin black line, the thickness depending upon the shaving to be removed. Incidentally, always try to keep the edge square with the side of the cutter. The jack plane cutter should be rounded in its length somewhat, whilst trying and smoothing plane cutters should be *very* slightly rounded, with the corners taken off. More detailed information on the care and maintenance of planes is given in the companion volume, *Tools for Woodwork*.

Block plane. This small plane (F, Fig. 8) comes in for many small jobs. Its small mouth makes it invaluable for trimming narrow wood which would simply fall into the larger mouth of a bigger plane. Its cutter is fixed with the bevel uppermost.

Compass plane. Those who go in for shaped work will find this an invaluable tool. Its sole can be set to either a convex or concave curve (see G, Fig. 8). In use it must always be pushed forward in line with the curve, not used with a slicing action.

SPECIAL PLANES

We now come to planes made for special purposes, and chief amongst them are those used for working or cleaning up rebates. They include the rebate plane (which may be of metal or wood), the shoulder plane, and the bullnose plane, both of metal. Of these the rebate plane is used for all general rebating.

Rebate plane. The metal type is provided with an adjustable fence and depth stop, in which form it is virtually a fillister plane. A spur is also fitted, the purpose of which is to cut the fibres when working across the grain. Being situated in front of the cutter it severs the grain before the cutter comes into action and so prevents splitting out. It is unnecessary for working *with* the grain and is then fixed in its neutral position.

Wooden rebate planes (H, Fig. 8) sometimes have a fence and stop (when they are known as a fillister plane) but for the greater part they are of the simple kind. When using the latter the fingers of the left hand should curl beneath the sole in a similar way to when the jack plane is used on an edge (see Fig. 9). Generally the safe plan is to begin with a narrow rebate, and, when a reasonable start has been made, widen it by laying the plane on its side. For cross-grain the width must be deeply gauged and a cut made with the chisel after every few shavings to prevent splitting out. When the rebate is extra deep the grain should be cut with the saw.

Shoulder plane. The shoulder plane (I, Fig. 8) is used mostly for trimming wide shoulders. Its low pitch and perfect accuracy make it specially suitable for end grain and close work. In the same class, but having a considerably greater variety of uses is the bullnose plane (K, Fig. 8). Apart from trimming small rebates it has a hundred and one general bench uses and is well worth its cost. An

FIG. 16. WORKING A GROOVE USING THE PLOUGH PLANE.
Either wood or metal plough planes can be obtained. The latter has the advantage of easy adjustment. Cutters are usually in sets of seven or eight.

essential feature of the sharpening of all three of the above planes is that the edge must be kept square.

Plough. For working grooves the plough plane (L, Fig. 8) is used, and many varieties are available. If you reckon to do just small work only the small metal type with three cutters, $\frac{1}{8}$ in., $\frac{3}{16}$ in., and $\frac{1}{4}$ in., is handy. It is, however, a light tool and the full-size plough with up to a dozen cutters is more useful. The wood plane plough is shown in use in Fig. 16.

Moulding planes. Owing to the use of the machine spindle moulder, hand moulding planes are not used much nowadays. When no machinery is available, however, they are still needed for

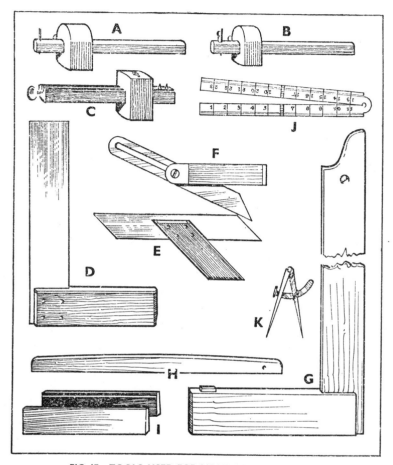

FIG. 17.   TOOLS USED FOR MARKING AND TESTING.

A. MARKING GAUGE.—For marking *with the* grain or for end grain.

B. CUTTING GAUGE.—For both cutting and marking in any direction of grain.

C. MORTISE GAUGE.—For marking the mortise and tenon joint.

D. TRY SQUARE.—For marking and testing. 6 in. and 12 in.

E. MITRE SQUARE.—For marking and testing mitres.   12 in.

F. SLIDING BEVEL.—For marking odd angles 9 in.

G. LARGE TRY SQUARE.—About 30 in.

H. STRAIGHT-EDGE.—About 3–5 ft.

I. WINDING STRIPS.—About 12 in.

J. RULE.—2 or 3 ft. folding rule.

K. DIVIDERS.—About 5 in.

larger and more elaborate mouldings. They should be obtained only as needed because many mouldings can be worked by means of the rebate plane and the scratch-stock.

Note that the plane is generally held at an angle (the exact angle is indicated on the front of the plane by a line which marks the vertical). English pattern planes are invariably made in this way, whilst French ones are generally made to be held upright. Always begin the moulding at the far end of the wood. Take off a few shavings and bring the plane back a little further at each stroke. This helps to prevent it from drifting with the grain. It will cease to cut automatically when the full depth is reached. It is obviously necessary to keep the fence pressed tightly up against the wood. Stone slips are used for sharpening the cutters, care being taken to keep them to the shape of the plane sole.

MARKING AND TESTING TOOLS
Gauges

These are extremely important because accurate work is almost impossible without them. Yet they invariably cause the beginner difficulty. The trouble is usually due to their not being held

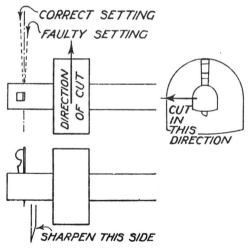

FIG. 18. CUTTER DETAIL OF CUTTING GAUGE.
If correctly set the gauge will tend to draw into the wood.

properly and sometimes (in the case of the cutting gauge) to incorrect sharpening.

Three kinds of gauges are available : the marking gauge, A, Fig. 17, which can be used for marking *with* the grain or on end grain ; the cutting gauge, B, which will mark in any direction, and will cut thin wood ; and the mortise gauge, C, used in marking the mortise and tenon joint. It is clear that of the first two the cutting gauge is the more useful, but since two gauges are desirable in cabinet work the usual plan is to have one cutting and one marking gauge. The advantage of having two is realised chiefly in such work as letting in hinges, in which one is used to mark the thickness and the other the width of the hinge.

Cutting gauge. It will be seen that the cutting gauge has a

FIG. 19. METHOD OF HOLDING THE CUTTING GAUGE.

In addition to downward pressure it is important that the fence of the gauge is pressed into the edge.

cutter held by a wedge. It is important to see that this is set properly, because, if it should incline in its width towards the fence, it will tend to drift away from the edge of the wood. It should be set if anything a trifle away from the parallel as in Fig. 18. Another point is that it should be sharpened with the bevel nearest the fence as this again helps to prevent drifting.

The method of holding the gauge is shown in Fig. 19. Note that the forward movement is provided chiefly by the thumb, the first finger gives a certain amount of downward pressure and helps to control the gauge, the second and third fingers press steadily inwards against the fence to prevent drifting, whilst the little finger can either rest with the others above the bar, or curl beneath as shown where it will help in keeping the gauge square. Remember that the inward pressure is vital in preventing the gauge from drifting away from the edge. When used for cutting thin wood the tool is used half-way in from each side.

Mortise gauge. The mortise gauge is used similarly. When setting, the adjustable cutter is moved so that the distance between it and the fixed cutter is exactly equal to the chisel width. The fence is then adjusted. Remember to use it from the face-side on both mortise and tenon.

Squares. These tools are used for both marking and testing and should be treated with respect. A fall to the ground is enough to put a square out of truth. The 6 in. size is the most generally useful since it is used for testing the squareness of edges when planing, marking shoulders, and a hundred and one other purposes.

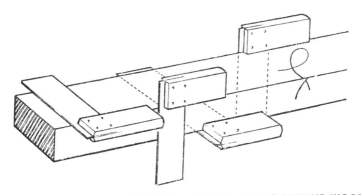

FIG. 20. TRY SQUARE POSITIONS WHEN SQUARING LINE AROUND WOOD.

This is to emphasise that the butt of the square is held always against either the face side or face edge of the wood. This ensures that the lines will meet when squared round.

When squaring a line right round all four sides of a piece of wood, as in marking a shoulder, always keep the butt against either the face-side or the face-edge. If this is done the lines will meet when squared round. Fig. 20 shows the idea. The same thing applies when testing wood whilst planing. The 12-in. (D, Fig. 17) square comes in for testing and marking panels, whilst the large wooden one (home-made), G, is for large work such as cabinet tops, wardrobe ends, etc.

Mitre square and bevel. The use of the mitre square, E, is similar to that of the try square except, of course, that it is set at 45 deg. and is used mostly in mitreing. Squares having both the 90-deg. and the 45-deg. angles can be obtained, but they are not so effective as the two separate tools.

The sliding bevel, F, is needed for odd angles. A simple example is the case of a knife box having sloping sides and mitred corners. The angles are compound, that is, they slope at odd angles in both width and thickness. Then again, the angles of, say, an octagonal box need to have the mitres set out with the adjustable bevel at an odd angle.

Parallel strips (or winding strips), I, are useful for testing whether a piece of wood is free from winding. They are used as in Fig. 21. They come in also for testing the legs of a chair or cabinet stand to see whether it will stand square without rocking. A straight-edge, H, is needed for some work, and a length of 3 to 5 ft. is useful. Both the last-named tools can be home made.

FIG. 21. TESTING WHETHER SURFACE IS FREE FROM WINDING.

The parallel strips are placed at the ends of the wood. If true the edges of the strips will appear parallel.

Rule. The 2- or 3-ft. folding type is the most serviceable (see J).

Dividers. The chief use of these, K, is in stepping out distances for dividing a length into an odd number of equal parts, and sometimes for scribing a circle.

CHISELS

For general bench work the firmer chisel (A, Fig. 22) is used. It is sturdily built so that it will stand up to fairly heavy work such as chopping dovetails, etc. You can start off with 1 in. and $\frac{1}{4}$ in. sizes, and obtain others as you need them. The $\frac{1}{4}$-in. one is handy for clearing out $\frac{5}{16}$ in. mortises (see later). It is always as well to set aside certain chisels which you will use for close, accurate work such as paring, and for this the bevelled-edge type (B) is excellent. It

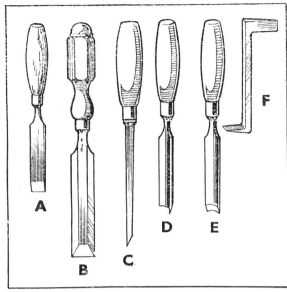

A. FIRMER CHISEL.—Strong chisel for chopping dovetails, etc., and general bench work. Useful sizes ¼ in., ½ in., ¾ in., 1 in.

B. BEVELLED-EDGE CHISEL.—For paring and fine work. Handy sizes, ¾ in. and 1¼ in. (extra long paring chisel).

C. SASH MORTISE CHISEL.—For mortising. Useful sizes, ¼ in., ⁵⁄₁₆ in., ⅜ in.

D. OUTSIDE GROUND GOUGE. — For working concave shapes. ½ in. size handy but select according to work in hand. Also known as firmer gouge.

E. INSIDE GROUND GOUGE.—For scribing mouldings, etc. Choose in accordance with work in hand Also known as scribing gouge.

F. DRAWER LOCK CHISEL.— For recessing drawer locks and chopping mortises of lock bolts, etc.

FIG. 22. CHISELS AND GOUGES.

will work closely into acute corners. Being a much slighter tool, however, it should never be used for chopping.

Using the chisel. Fig. 23 shows a groove being pared with the bevelled-edge chisel. Note specially how the fingers of the left hand guide and steady the blade. Also, and still more important, how they are *behind* the cutting edge. This is a golden rule applying to all edge tools, and observance of it will prevent many an accident. For the final cuts the tool can be worked with a slicing movement. This helps in making the work flat and eases the cutting.

A typical chopping operation is shown in Fig. 24, that of cutting dovetails. Note that the work is handscrewed down over a solid part of the bench and that a piece of waste wood is placed beneath. In such work the chisel should never be placed directly on the line at the start because, owing to its wedge shape, the blade is liable to be forced past the line. Start it about $\frac{1}{16}$ in. from the line, and bring it right up to the latter only when making the final cut.

Mortising. This involves some heavy chopping work and a strong chisel is therefore needed. Two patterns are available, the heavy mortise type and the sash mortise. The latter (Fig. 22, C) is suitable for cabinet work, being rather lighter than the other. Choose the $\frac{5}{16}$ in. size to begin with because this is the most suitable width for mortises in 1-in. and ⅞-in. stuff. Most frames and doors are in one of these thicknesses. Fig. 25 shows a mortise being chopped. A great deal of the waste is removed first by boring with a bit slightly smaller than the mortise width.

Another type of chisel coming in for occasional use is the drawer-lock chisel, F, Fig. 22. It is frequently difficult or even impossible to use an ordinary chisel owing to there being insufficient room for the handle, let alone room to strike it. The cranked-type chisel enables the recess to be cut without difficulty, as shown in Fig. 26.

FIG. 23. PARING GROOVE USING BEVELLED-EDGE CHISEL.

The chisel is given a slicing movement, partly to ease the cutting, and partly because it helps in making the surface flat.

All chisels are sharpened similarly to plane irons (see page 14) The important point is to avoid dubbing over the edge when removing the burr. As a general rule paring chisels can be sharpened at a rather more acute angle than those for heavier work. The thinner edge enables the tool to slice more easily through the wood. It would not be practicable for a firmer chisel, however, because the edge would be liable to crumble with the strain.

Gouges. Gouges are not widely used in cabinet work, but they are needed occasionally. The best plan is to buy the gouge for the job as it comes along. Two kinds are available, the firmer or out-side-ground gouge, D, and the paring or inside-ground type, E. The former comes in for general bench work and has the advantage of being easily sharpened by a rocking movement on the oilstone. The paring gouge, used for such work as scribing mouldings, etc.,

FIG. 24. CHOPPING DOVETAILS.

The work is cramped down on to a solid part of the bench. Start short of the gauge line, and make the final cut right on the line. This joint is the secret mitre dovetail, but when through dovetails are being cut the waste should be sawn away first up to within about $\frac{1}{16}$ in. of the gauge line, the coping saw being used.

FIG. 25. CHOPPING A MORTISE.

Note that, in addition to being cramped down, a thumbscrew is put across the wood to prevent splitting. Much of the waste can be bored away first. Put the work over a solid part of the bench.

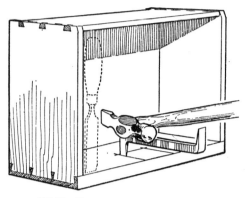

FIG. 26. THE DRAWER-LOCK CHISEL.

needs the use of the oilstone slip. Since it takes considerable time to sharpen it should be used with respect and kept for fine finishing cuts only.

BRACE AND BITS

The extra cost of the ratchet brace (A, Fig. 28) is well worth while because it can be used in a corner or close up to a surface where the sweep of the plain brace would prevent it from being revolved. What happens is that movement of the handle in one direction revolves the bit, whilst the back swing leaves it stationary. Thus a hole can be bored by merely moving the handle through half or even a quarter of its sweep. The ratchet can be made to work in either direction.

Bits. Chief amongst the bits is the twist (Fig. 28, B). Its main virtue is that it will not drift with the grain (a special advantage in end grain). It is thus suitable for deep holes such as in dowelling. The first two sizes you want are the $\frac{3}{8}$ in. and the $\frac{1}{4}$ in. The former is the usual size for dowelling $\frac{7}{8}$-in. and 1-in. wood, and a specially short bit for the purpose is made. The $\frac{1}{4}$ in. size, apart from dowelling thinner stuff, is invaluable for boring holes in mortises to help clear the waste before using the chisel. Larger sizes are needed eventually, but they can be obtained as occasion arises. Use a fine file with a safe edge for sharpening. Take special care not to damage the thread, and avoid dubbing over the edges. Fig. 27

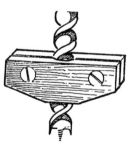

FIG. 27. HOME-MADE DEPTH STOP FOR TWIST BIT.

shows how a depth stop can be made easily in wood when a number of holes have to be bored all to the same depth.

Centre bits. The centre bit (E) is mostly for shallow holes. It is seldom successful in end grain owing to there being nothing to prevent it from drifting. It is sharpened with a fine file. Retain the same sharpening bevel and be careful not to dub over the under-side of the cutter or the outside of the nicker. Some modern centre bits have a thread in place

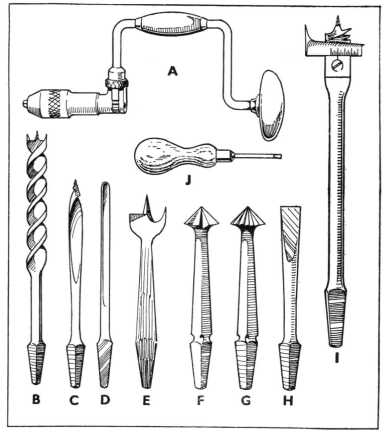

FIG. 28. TYPES OF BORING TOOLS.

A. RATCHET BRACE.—Can be used in awkward corners. 8 in. or 10 in. sweep is useful all-round size.

B. TWIST BIT.—For deep holes which must be true, as in dowelling. Useful sizes ¼ in., ⅜ in., ½ in., ⅝ in.

C. HALF-TWIST BIT.—Quick and easy cutting but liable to split the wood. ¼ in.

D. SHELL BIT.—For screw holes. ⅛ in. and ₁³₆ in.

DRILL BIT.—For screw holes. Quicker cutting than the shell bit. ⅛ in. and ₁³₆ in.

E. CENTRE BIT.—Used mostly for shallow holes. ½ in., ¾ in., 1 in.

F. SNAIL COUNTERSINK.—For recessing screw heads. ½ in.

G. ROSE COUNTERSINK.—For brass, ½ in.

H. TURNSCREW BIT.—For quick driving and when great leverage is needed.

I. EXPANSION BIT.—Can be adjusted to bore various sizes of large holes.

J. BRADAWL.—Used mostly for screw holes. About ₃³₂ in. and ⅛ in.

of the pointed centre. This makes them less laborious in use as the thread draws them into the wood. Be careful to avoid nails when boring because a jar on the thread may entirely ruin the bit.

C.M.F.B.—3

FIG. 29. USE OF TWIST BIT WHEN DOWELLING.

Note that the worker stands at the end of the wood. It is easier to judge whether the brace bears to the right or left than whether it leans away from or towards you. A depth gauge is fitted to the bit.

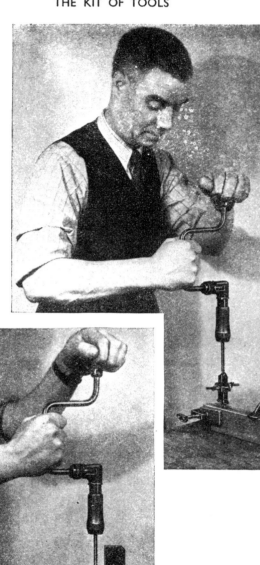

FIG. 30. BORING END OF LEG FOR DOWEL.

A straight-edge is cramped to the leg as a guide to keeping the brace upright. If necessary a second straight-edge can be fixed to the adjacent side.

Bits for screwing. A variety of bits is available for screw and similar holes. These include the shell, spoon, nose, half-twist, and drill bits. A snail countersink, F, is needed for sinking screw heads flush ; the rose type, G, is sometimes needed when the holes in brass fittings need enlarging. The expansion bit, I, is handy occasionally, but it can be bought later. The great advantage is that it saves having to keep a wide range of centre bits. Others, such as the turnscrew bit, reamer, and so on can also follow.

Using the brace. A try square can be used as an indication whether the brace is being held upright. Remember, however, that it is fairly easy to tell whether it leans to the right or left. The difficulty is to know whether it is tilting away from or towards you. In important cases it is as well to ask some one to stand at the side and indicate whether you are holding the brace upright. A safeguard in such jobs as dowelling and the preliminary boring in mortising is always to stand at the end of the work rather than at the side (the position is shown in Fig. 29). The point is that if the hole should lean slightly in the direction of the length of the wood it would not matter so much as if it were to slope towards the side. Fig. 30 shows how a straight-edge cramped to the work enables you to judge the verticality on an important job such as boring for a dowel at the end of a leg or other similar item.

An important tool for boring small screw holes, etc., is the bradawl (J, Fig. 28). Two kinds are available, the more usual round-sectioned form, and the square or bird-cage maker's awl. The latter has the advantage of not being liable to split the wood when used near the edge. The round awl should always have its cutting edge at right angles with the grain so that it cuts rather than forces its way into the grain as a wedge.

VARIOUS TOOLS

The purpose and use of most of these tools is obvious. One special note we may give is in connection with the oilstone. Do not buy a cheap one ; it will inevitably give trouble in the long run. A good one will cut as well in ten years' time as now ; a cheap one may gum up and be useless in as many weeks. Treat it properly however. Use the kind of oil recommended by the maker, and make a box for it. Remember that it will not survive many falls. When sharpening a chisel or other narrow tool keep it moving over all parts of the surface, in particular along the sides, because the tendency of a stone is to become hollow in use. After use wipe off the old dirty oil.

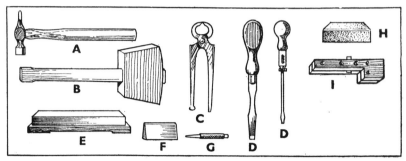

FIG. 31. GENERAL BENCH TOOLS IN EVERYDAY USE.

A. HAMMER.—Warrington pattern. For normal use, about 8 oz. head.
HAMMER.—Pattern maker's. For fine pins, about 3 oz. head.
B. MALLET.—For use with chisels. About 6 in. head.
C. PINCERS.—8 in.
D. SCREWDRIVERS.—8 in. blade, for large screws. 5 in. small ratchet screwdriver, for small screws.
E. OILSTONE.—*India, Carborundum, Aloxite,* or *Washita,* etc. " Fine " grade, or combination " Coarse " and " Fine." Size 8 in. by 2 in.
F. OILSTONE SLIP.—For sharpening gouges, spokeshaves, etc., " Fine " grade. Makes as above. Useful size 4 in. by 1 in.
G. PUNCHES.—Small hollow-centre punch for fine pins ; larger one for big nails.
H. CORK RUBBER.—For glasspapering. About 4½ in. by 2½ in.
I. SCRATCH-STOCK.—For working mouldings and inlay grooves, etc. Home made. About 7 in. by 2½ in. by 1½ in.

The scratch-stock, I, Fig. 31, is a home-made tool and is used for working small mouldings and in inlaying. It consists of a block of wood with a notch cut in it and then sawn in two in its thickness. The cutter is an odd strip of steel such as an old saw blade filed to the required size and shape. It is held between the thicknesses by tightening the screws and is simply worked back and forth along the edge of the wood as in Fig. 32. The projection of the cutter is so arranged that it ceases to cut when the full depth is reached. An essential feature of its use is that it is kept tightly up against the edge of the wood. In section the edge of the notch is slightly rounded.

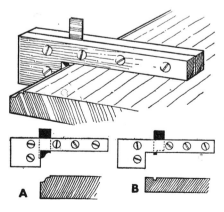

FIG. 32. USE OF SCRATCH-STOCK.

This is useful for both mouldings and inlay grooves. Its special value is when the moulding or groove has to be stopped since it need not be taken right through.

You will note that for the small screwdriver a ratchet is advised. The advantage of this will be felt when hinging a door. The left hand has to hold the door so that one hand only is available. By using the ratchet it is merely necessary to rock the wrist back and forth whilst a constant pressure is maintained. The screwdriver need never leave the screw slot until the screw is right in.

SPOKESHAVES, RASP, AND FILE

As in the case of planes, spokeshaves are made in both wood and metal, and opinion as to their respective merits varies. Their use is that of truing and smoothing shaped edges after sawing. Some are made with a flat face for dealing with convex shapes, whilst others have a round face making them suitable for hollow curves. Their use is similar. The purpose should be to remove any lumps first and then work the tool in long even strokes, taking care to hold it at right angles. Always work *with* the grain.

Sharpening. The metal type, B, Fig. 33, is sharpened similarly

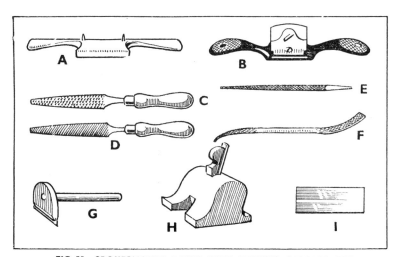

FIG. 33. SPOKESHAVES, RASPS, FILES, ROUTER, SCRAPER, ETC.

A. WOOD SPOKESHAVE.—For finishing shaped edges. In beech or (preferably) boxwood. Useful size 2¼ in. cutter.

B. METAL SPOKESHAVE.—With round face for concave shapes, and flat face for convex curves. 2 in. cutter.

C. WOOD RASP.—Similar to the file but cuts more quickly and gives coarser finish. Half-round, about 7 in. long.

D. WOOD FILE.—For removing saw marks

from shaped edges, etc. Half-round, about 7 in. long.

E. RAT TAIL FILE.—For acute concave shapes. About ¼ in. diameter tapering to end.

F. RIFFLER.—Available in various shapes and used chiefly for compound shapes.

G. VENEERING HAMMER.—About 7 in.

H. ROUTER.—Wood or Metal

I. SCRAPER.—About 5 in. Also with curved edge.

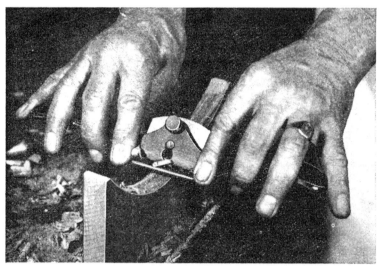

FIG. 34. CLEANING UP A SHAPE WITH THE METAL SPOKESHAVE.
This is fitted with a cutter similarly to a plane, except that there is no back iron. Some kinds are adjustable.

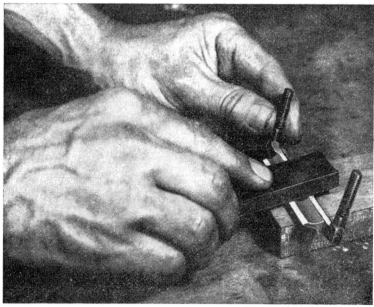

FIG. 35. SHARPENING THE WOOD SPOKESHAVE CUTTER.
A small oilstone slip can conveniently be used.

to a plane iron (see page 14), but, since it is small, it is an excellent idea to make a simple holder for it as shown in Fig. 37. It is a plain block of wood with a saw kerf in it in which the cutter fits.

The wood spokeshave cutter, A, cannot be sharpened in this way, owing to the projecting tangs. Either the edge of the oilstone or an oilstone slip must be used. Fig. 35 shows the process. The

FIG. 36. FOLLOWING THE GRAIN WHEN SPOKE-
SHAVING.

Study the grain beforehand so that the tool always cuts
with the grain as shown by the arrows.

under-edge is rubbed until a burr is turned up. Avoid the temptation of tilting the slip in order to produce an edge more quickly. There is no need to do so because the cutter is hollow ground like a razor. When a keen edge has been formed the burr can be removed by rubbing the face of the cutter flat on the stone, but many workers prefer not to turn back the burr as it helps the tool to cut. Avoid dubbing over the edge.

Rasp and file. Used also for cleaning up curved edges, etc. are the rasp, C, and file, D. They are particularly handy in work for which the spokeshave would be impossible—in very quick curves and in working close up to a corner, for instance. The rasp is the coarser of the two and is used only when there are deep saw marks or other inequalities to be taken out. In many cases the file only is needed.

Generally the most effective way of using the tool (either of them) is to give both a forward and sideways movement simultaneously. The actual cutting is done by the forward movement, but by rocking sideways the continuity of the curve is the better preserved. Normally the rasp is used first to bring the shape practically down to the line, the file

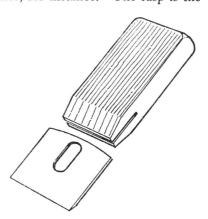

FIG. 37. HOLDER FOR CUTTER.

The iron spokeshave cutter is too small to be
gripped easily, hence the use of this holder.

follows to remove the coarse marks of the rasp, and the file marks are taken out by the scraper. Finally the edge is glasspapered, a rubber being used over the glasspaper to prevent the edges from being dubbed over. For very acute concave curves the rat-tail file, E, is handy. It comes in also for enlarging holes. When shapes are compound the riffler, F, is useful. Many wood shapers are now available which largely replace the rasp, and are non-clogging.

Router. This can be obtained in either wood (H, Fig. 33) or in metal. The former has a high-pitched cutter which has more of a scraping than a cutting action. It is used for making a groove of equal depth throughout after the bulk of the waste has been chiselled.

The veneering hammer, G, is generally home made and is used for pressing down veneer (see page 115). The scraper, I, is dealt with more particularly below.

SCRAPER

This all-important tool is essential to good cabinet work, yet its correct sharpening and use eludes most beginners. Its purpose is to take out marks left by the plane, and to remove tears (pronounced " tares ") in the grain. In veneering it is essential because the thinness of the veneer would not permit the use of the plane. It is used as shown in Fig. 39, the thumbs pressing in the centre and so giving the scraper a slight bow shape. After a short period of use it becomes unbearably hot so that the user is glad to change to the

FIG. 38. TWO KINDS OF SCRAPERS AND ENLARGED SECTION OF EDGE.
The normal rectangular pattern is given at A. That at B is used for shaped work. C shows how the edges are turned up.

other edge. Most cabinet makers develop blisters on their thumbs as a result of continued scraping. It will be seen from C, Fig. 38, that the corners are turned over to a hook shape (shown in exaggeration), and it is these which cut the wood. Actual fine shavings should be produced ; dust is useless.

Sharpening. The first job in sharpening is make the edges straight and square, and the preliminary rubbing down is done with a flat file, the scraper being held in the vice. To remove the file marks the edge is next rubbed on the oilstone until all file scratches have disappeared. Hold it in a rag to prevent the hand from being injured. Each side in turn is then rubbed flat on the stone. This makes all four corners sharp and square, and it remains to turn up the edges. Hold the scraper flat on the bench with the edge over-hanging slightly. Select a hard rounded instrument such as a gouge and, holding it at a *slight* angle to the scraper, draw it smartly along with a fair pressure, first in one direction and then in the other as in Fig. 40. This should turn up an edge which can be detected

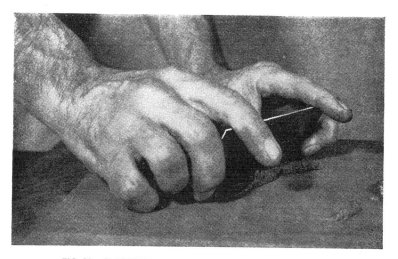

FIG. 39. CLEANING UP A SURFACE WITH THE SCRAPER.

Pressure is applied with the thumbs. This slightly bends the scraper and prevents the corners from digging in. In some cases it is an advantage to hold the tool askew.

by drawing the thumb across the corners. Treat all four edges in the same way. Some prefer to hold the scraper upright on the bench, and draw the gouge upwards.

When the edges become dull they can be restored by rubbing down the burrs. Hold the scraper flat on the bench and draw the gouge along the surface flat upon it. It is then just a matter of turning them afresh. The scraper can be sharpened several times in this way, but eventually it will fail to hold an edge and it becomes necessary to rub down again with file and oilstone.

The angle at which the tool is held is found by experience. Some-times it can be more effectively used by skewing it round somewhat so that it has somewhat of a slicing movement. This is especially desirable when cleaning up crossbandings and other parts where the grain runs at an odd angle.

Kinds of scrapers. Scrapers are made in various sizes and thicknesses. A 5 in. length is a good average size (A, Fig. 38). The thickness should be somewhere about $\frac{3}{64}$ in. A thinner one than this is liable to become very hot, whilst a thick one is stiff, offering considerable resistance to bending, and so being tiring in use.

A second kind of scraper, curved in shape as at B, Fig. 38, is used in shaped work. It is sharpened with the gouge similarly to the

FIG. 40. TURNING UP THE SCRAPER EDGE WITH A GOUGE.
Note that the gouge is held at a slight angle so that the corner is turned back. After being so sharpened a few times the scraper needs to be rubbed down afresh.

straight type. Its uses are limited, and there is no need to obtain it until it is actually required.

VARIOUS APPLIANCES

For sawing mitres the mitre block, A, Fig. 41, and mitre box, B, are used, the former for small work and the other for large mitres. It is a good plan also to make two extra cuts, one at right angles and the other at $67\frac{1}{2}$ deg. The latter is useful in that it is the mitring

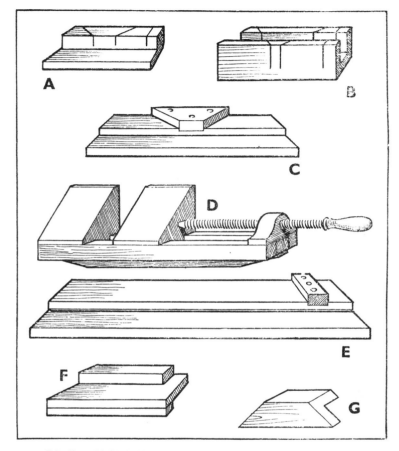

FIG. 41. APPLIANCES FOR SAWING, PLANING, AND CHISELLING.

A. MITRE BLOCK.—For small mouldings. About 9 in.

B. MITRE BOX.—To take large mouldings up to 3 in. or more according to work.

C. MITRE SHOOTING BOARD.—For trimming mitre. About 18 in.

D. MITRE SHOOTING BLOCK.—For trimming mitres and square ends.

E. SHOOTING BOARD.—For planing joints in thin wood, and trimming square ends. About 2 ft., also about 5 ft.

F. BENCH HOOK.—To hold wood whilst sawing on bench. About 9 in. by 8 in.

G. MITRE TEMPLATE.—For chiselling mitres on door frames in which moulding is worked in the solid. About 4½ in. by 1½ in. by 1½ in.

angle for pieces which join at 135 deg. ; that is, a right angle plus 45 deg.

For trimming mitres the mitre shooting-board, C, can be used for small sections. For large mouldings the mitre shooting-block, D, is better. This appliance also has a square surface. It is advisable to glue a piece of thin card over the working faces to prevent shavings from being removed accidentally.

The mitre template, G, is used for chiselling the mitres of mouldings worked in the solid on doors, frames, etc.   Fig. 42 shows it in use where it will be seen that the chisel lies flat on the mitre surface, this giving it the exact slope at which to cut.   It is easily made at home.

Mention has been made of the shooting-board (page 13).   It is

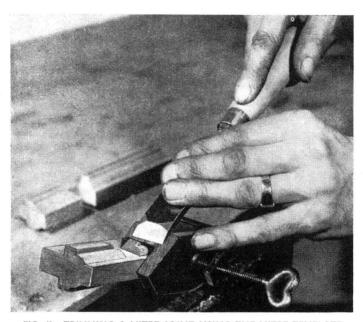

FIG. 42. TRIMMING A MITRE JOINT USING THE MITRE TEMPLATE.

The ends of the template are at 45 deg., and the chisel blade lies flat so that it is guided at the correct angle.

shown at E, Fig. 41.   Two are desirable, one about 2 ft. long for trimming small pieces and for shooting short joints, and a large one for long joints.   It is a good plan to plane true the underside of both to enable them to be used for planing boards.   Details of a bench hook are given at F.   Note that the lower piece at the front which bears against the bench is dowelled on.   This is because the saw might otherwise jar on any nails or screws used for fixing.

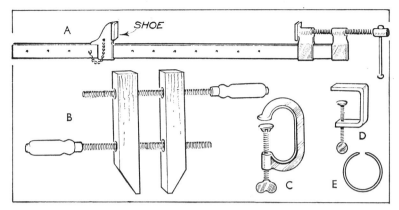

FIG. 43. VARIOUS TYPES OF CRAMPS.

A. SASH CRAMPS.—To take work up to 24 in. Pair usually needed. Also pair to take work up to 42 in.

B. HANDSCREWS.—Chop size about 8 in.

C. G CRAMPS.—To take work up to 8 in.

D. THUMBSCREWS.—2½–4 in.

E. SPRING DOGS.—For cramping awkward shapes. About 4 in. diameter.

SPRING CLOTHES PEGS.— For holding down beads, etc., whilst glue sets.

CRAMPS

These are required mostly for making tight joints though they have their uses in holding down wood whilst being worked. Sash cramps, A, are for pulling up doors and frames, carcases, and so on. A pair of each size is desirable. Wooden bar cramps are alternatives, but are not used much nowadays. These should always be used with a waste block of wood beneath the screw to avoid marking. Handscrews, B, are an excellent form of cramp. In use the chops are opened the required amount and the first screw tightened. The second screw is then turned so that it levers over the jaw and exerts great pressure. By suitably adjusting the first screw the pressure can be localised where required. G-cramps, C, are an alternative. Thumbscrews, D, are for similar purposes but are used for small work.

Sometimes it is awkward for one reason or another to use any of the above cramps, especially when the work is of an awkward shape. Spring dogs, E, can then often be used. Similar cramps can often be cut from old upholstery springs. They are particularly useful in repair work and for light jobs. Clothes pegs of the spring type too are handy. They do not exert much pressure, but their chief value is in holding down parts (such as light mouldings, etc.) which would be liable to spring whilst the glue sets.

MACHINES FOR CABINET MAKING

It is obvious that machinery is being used ever increasingly in woodwork. Even the few remaining " hand " craftsmen use machines to an extent.   In fact any man who buys a board has used a machine in the sense that a machine saw was used to cut it from the log.   This has to be accepted, and the economics of the trade are such that machines have to be used, at least for all basic operations. It follows then that any man who makes furniture should be familiar with the function of machines, their uses, and indeed, their limitations.

FIG. 44. SMALL BENCH CIRCULAR SAW.

The machine has a 10-in. saw, and is powered by a 1-h.p. motor. The spindle revolves at 3,000 r.p.m.

When a machine will perform an operation better than, or at least as well as, hand work there seems no logical reason against its use, especially when it does it in a tithe of the time.   It is only when a machine is used for economic reasons in the knowledge that the result will be inferior, or when the standard of design has to be lowered to enable a machine to be used that the real trouble begins.

When it is practicable to install separate machines for individual operations it is an advantage to do so because a machine is invariably more efficient when designed for a single purpose.   If lack of space or other reason makes this impracticable, the universal machine or the type of machine which is basically a lathe but with various attachments is an excellent alternative.

We follow here with a brief review of the smaller basic machines, their essential features, and the work they will do.   Those seeking fuller information should see *Light Machines for Woodwork* in this series, or other similar text-books.

CIRCULAR SAW AND BANDSAW

	Essential or desirable features	Operations
CIRCULAR SAW.	Rise-and-fall table or saw. Enables grooving, rebating, and tenoning to be done. Tilting table or saw. Angle cuts can be made. Draw plate in table. Gives clearance when angle cutting or using wobble saw. Mitre gauge. Essential for cross-cutting, mitreing, dimension cutting, etc. Riving Knife. Prevents binding due to kerf closing on saw. Top and bottom guard. Former adjustable in height. Latter usually formed by main casting.	Used for ripping or cross-cutting, mitreing, compound angles, tenoning, grooving, rebating, and in some cases permits use of Whitehill cutter block. Grooving has generally to be taken right through, though a long stop can be arranged, length of which varies with saw diameter. The smaller the saw the shorter the stop.
BANDSAW.	Tilting table, preferably with groove for mitre gauge. Tracking adjustment, enabling saw position on wheels to be maintained or adjusted. Thrust wheel desirable below as well as above table; also adjustable guides. Top thrust wheel and guide unit should be adjustable in height. Tensioning device essential.	Chiefly used for cutting shapes, but can be used for both ripping and cross-cutting though is not so efficient as the circular saw. Cross-cutting is limited by throat clearance. Tenoning and deep sawing can be done; also angle sawing when table tilts. Cannot be used for grooving, rebating, or internal cuts.

(By courtesy Coronet Tool Co. Ltd.)

FIG. 45. GROOVING ON MORTISING ATTACHMENT USING ROTARY MILLER BIT.
The same bit can be used for mortising but leaves rounded ends to mortise.

	Essential or desirable features	Operations
JIG SAW.	Various kinds available, continuous band type, spring plunger, or bow-spring return kind. Table should preferably tilt.	Chief use for internal cuts. Can be used for external cuts but is not so efficient as the bandsaw. Is relatively slow cutting.
PLANER.	Can be simple edger or combined surfacer and thicknesser. Small edgers or surfacers can usually have thicknessing attachment. Width of table controls width of wood that can be planed. Rebating table is an advantage. Cutters should be capable of individual adjustment. Fence should be free to tilt. Guard is essential. Thicknessing attachment for surfacer is desirable.	Surfacer or edger can be used to plane surfaces or edges up to limit of table width. Thicknessing can be done only on thicknesser, or on edger when thicknessing attachment is available. Rebating can be done up to width of table, depth is limited by casting of bearing. Rebates can be stopped but ends are rounded. Can also be used for stop or through chamfering, tapering, and open side recessing.
SPINDLE MOULDER.	Can have French head, slotted collars, square block, drunken saw or Whitehill cutter block. Rise-and-fall spindle essential.	Will cut grooves, rebates, or mouldings. Ends can be stopped but will run out in a curve to be hand finished. French head has the advantage that the cutter is ground to an exact reverse of the required section.

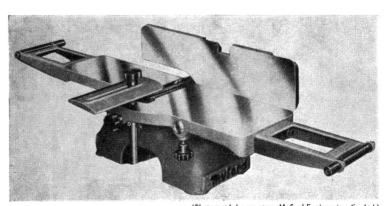

(Photograph by courtesy Myford Engineering Co. Ltd.)

FIG. 46.   BENCH PLANER WITH 4½ IN. CUTTER BLOCK.

The machine has three cutters and operates at 4,000 R.P.M. giving 12,000 cuts per minute off, has extension rollers, and a thicknessing attachment is available.

ROUTER AND SANDERS

	Essential or desirable features	Operations
ROUTER.	Can be large-production machine or small portable tool. High speed essential, 10,000–20,000 r.p.m.	Used for recessing, grooving, rebating, or moulding. High speed enables cut to be against grain without tearing out.
		Use of jigs enables repeat work to be done.
		All internal corners are rounded, diameter of bit controlling curve.
SANDERS.	Chief types: Disc.	Used for trimming squares mitres, etc., rather than for cleaning up.
	Belt.	For cleaning up. Abrasion marks run in straight line. Pressure applied locally with pad.
	Drum.	Large machine for production work, or small one with inflated head to give to shape being cleaned.

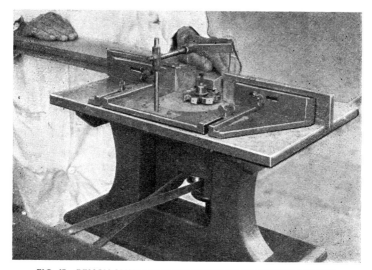

FIG. 47. BENCH SPINDLE MOULDER WITH GROOVING CUTTER.
This is the *AHOR* machine which can be fitted with the French head, slotted collars, or drunken saw.

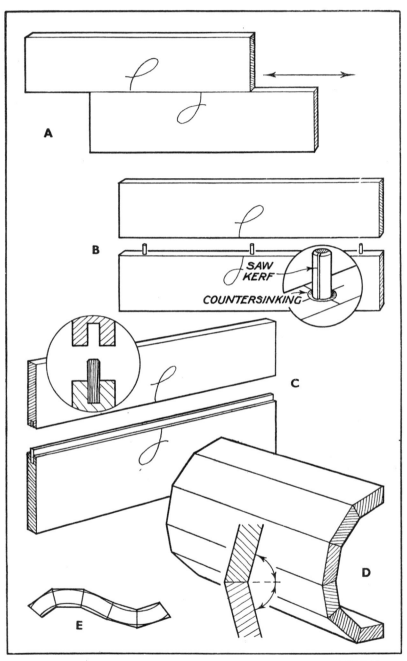

FIG. 1. GLUED AND COOPERED JOINTS, AND WAYS OF STRENGTHENING.

CHAPTER II. JOINTS

GLUED OR BUTT JOINTS, Fig. 1

Glued joints, A. These are used for jointing timber in its width. Lengths up to about 3 ft. can be glued and rubbed only (see arrows), but cramps are advisable for longer joints. Those to be rubbed should make a close fit throughout their length. At all costs avoid a rounded joint. When pivoted there should be definite friction at the ends. Cramped joints should be shot a trifle hollow and the cramps put in the middle. Glued joints are satisfactory for all woods which hold glue well, but other woods should be strengthened as shown opposite. Wood $\frac{3}{4}$ in. thick or more can be planed in the vice, but thinner wood (unless quite short) should be jointed on the shooting-board. Remember that one piece should be face-side uppermost and the other face-side downwards. This ensures the two being in alignment when assembled. Thick wood ($\frac{1}{2}$ in. or more) can be glued in the vice. Thinner wood should be rubbed together lying flat on two battens on the bench. Pieces of paper beneath the joint will prevent them from sticking.

Dowelled glued joint, B. Dowels can be used to strengthen the glued joint. For $\frac{7}{8}$-in. wood use $\frac{3}{8}$-in. dowels, two or more according to length. Countersink the holes slightly and round over the ends of the dowels. The length of the latter should be tested against the hole as they may otherwise prevent the joint from going home. A pencil dropped into the hole and offered against the dowel will show this. Avoid a large gap at the bottom of the hole. Note the saw kerf to allow surplus glue to escape when the dowels are knocked in.

Tongued and grooved joint, C. This is easily the strongest form of butt or glued joint, but has a disadvantage for some work in that the tongue shows at the ends. Use a tongue about $\frac{3}{16}$ in. thick for $\frac{7}{8}$-in. wood. Both this and the dowelled joint must be cramped. The tongue is cross-grained and should be a hand-tight fit. If too tight it will force open the groove.

Coopered joints, D. For shaped work the coopered joint is useful. It is virtually the same as the plain glued joint, but is at an angle. It is advisable to make a cradle for assembling, this being the inner shape of the job. It ensures the parts being at the correct angle and supports them whilst the glue sets.

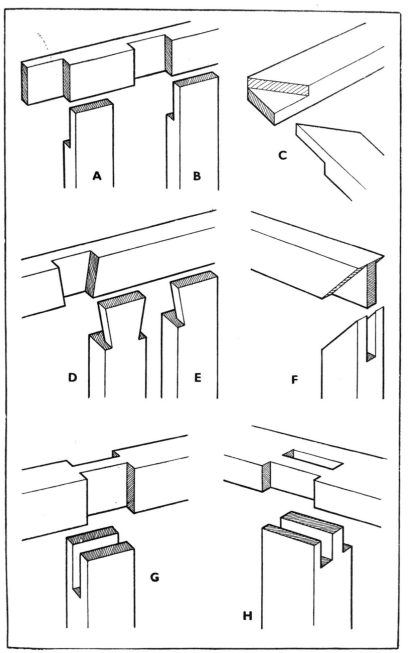

FIG. 2. HALVED AND BRIDLE JOINTS.

HALVED OR BRIDLE JOINTS, Fig. 2

Simple halving, A and B. Probably the simplest way of joining two pieces at right angles. It is not so strong as the mortise and tenon joint and requires nailing or screwing as well as gluing, but it is useful for light frames, etc. A is the end or *L* halving, and B the middle or *T* halving. The depth is marked with the gauge in both joints, this being used from the face side on both pieces. It is an advantage to use the chisel when squaring in the width of the joint. This enables a small sloping groove to be cut on the waste side, so forming a channel in which the saw can run. The advantage is that the chisel makes for accuracy and gives a cleaner joint line. When sawing down the gauge line of the end halving, A, keep the saw on the waste side. Otherwise the joint will not be level. In the case of the *T* halving at B, make this a hand-tight fit. If too tight it will probably bend the wood.

Mitred halving, C. This is neater than the simple *L* halving, and is specially useful when the surface has to be moulded. It is stronger than the plain mitre. Screws can be driven in from the back. If the top edges are moulded the moulding must not extend down beyond the line of the halving.

Dovetailed halving, D and E. Used when the dovetailed piece has to resist direct outward strain. The bare-faced dovetail at E is a simpler alternative. Cut the halving of the upright piece first and slope in the dovetail sides. Lay in position on the other piece and mark the sides. Saw down on the waste side.

Mitred bridle, F. Of special value in mirror frames, etc. Surface can be moulded. If a rebate has to be worked the slot must be set in by the rebate depth because the rebating automatically cuts away the tenon.

Bridle joint, G and H. One of the most useful applications of this is in the joint between the centre leg of a sideboard and the top rail. When the rail is upright the joint at G is used. H is for a rail which lies flat. The marking out is similar to that of the mortise and tenon joint. Remember to hold the saw on the waste side for every cut.

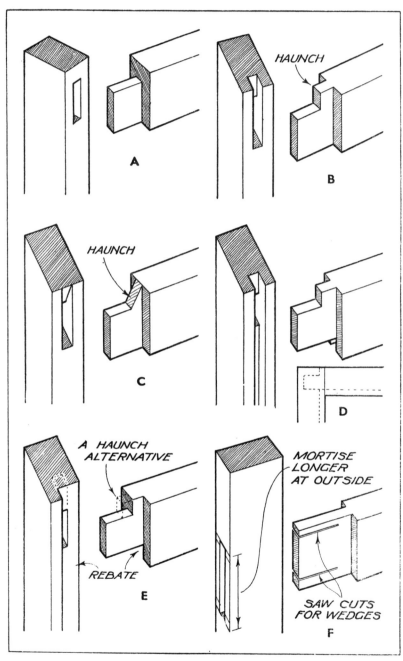

FIG. 3. MORTISE AND TENON JOINTS USED FOR DOORS, ETC.

MORTISE AND TENON JOINTS, Fig. 3

Stub-tenon, A. This has a wide variety of applications for doors, frames, and so on. The mortise is not chopped right through the wood but is taken through as far as is reasonably safe. If the rail joins the stile near the middle instead of at the end the tenon can be the full width of the wood. Alternatively, it can be set in slightly at both sides, thus concealing all traces of the mortise.

In all tenoned joints the thickness of the tenon should be about one-third that of the wood. Choose a mortise chisel that is nearest to the size. Thus, for $\frac{7}{8}$-in. wood use a $\frac{5}{16}$-in. chisel, and $\frac{1}{4}$-in. for $\frac{3}{4}$-in. wood. The tenon should make a hand-tight fit. It should be glued straight from the saw because the roughness gives a key to the glue. If any fitting is necessary use the file to roughen the tenon afresh. In mortising, much of the waste can be removed by first boring with a bit slightly smaller than the mortise width. Be careful to keep the brace upright.

Haunched tenon, B, C, and D. Similar to the stub-tenon but with a haunch left at the set-in of the tenon to resist any twisting tendency at the edge. The haunch at C is similar, but is entirely concealed when the joint is assembled. In the case of a grooved framework a haunch is always needed to fill in the end of the groove, D. Note too that the tenon must also be set in at the inside to an extent equal to the groove depth because the grooving automatically cuts away the tenon.

Long and short shoulder tenon, E. When a framework is rebated at the inside the back shoulder must be cut longer than the front one by the depth of the rebate. Note how it is also set in at the rebated edge by the rebate depth since the rebating necessarily cuts away the tenon. A haunch can be allowed as shown by dotted lines, if preferred. It is always an advantage in this type of joint to let the side of the tenon line up with the rebate.

Through mortise and tenon, F. Where strength is of great importance the tenon can be taken right through and wedged outside, the mortise being cut full at the outside. If the rail occurs at the end of the stile the tenon must be set in at the outside.

Mitred shoulder mortise and tenon. See page 57.

All these joints can be wholly or partly machine cut, but unless a suitable machine is available, it is advisable to cut shoulders by hand. This means that all shoulder lines must be squared in, but the tenon marks need be gauged in on one joint only, as the rest are automatically cut alike. See other notes in Chapter IV.

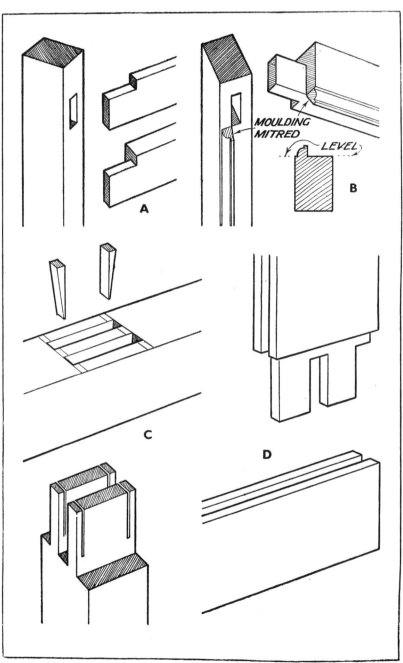

MOULDING
MITRED

LEVEL

A

B

C

D

FIG. 4. MORTISE AND TENON JOINTS FOR DOORS, FRAMES, ETC.

MORTISE AND TENON JOINTS, Fig. 4 (*continued*)

Barefaced tenon, A. If the rail is thinner than the stile the tenon need have no shoulders at the sides at all. Instead, a shoulder can be cut at the edge as in the top example at A. Except in the case of slats fitted to a framework it is always desirable to cut a shoulder of some sort because only in this way can the exact rail length be fixed. The mortise must be neatly cut because there are no side shoulders to conceal any gaps. When the rail is thicker a shoulder can be cut at one side only as in the lower example at A. The top-edge shoulder is an advantage in any case as it effectually conceals the mortise. Furthermore, it enables the top edges to be rounded without planing away the tenon corners.

Mortise and tenon for moulded and rebated frame, B. The shoulders are level since the rebate is level with lower quirk of the moulding, the latter being cut away locally opposite the mortise. The moulding is worked in the solid and the ends mitred, the mitre template being used (see page 37). The order in which the work is done is: mortise and tenon are cut; rebate worked; moulding planed; shoulders cut; mitre cut and joint fitted. When making a door the shoulder length is taken from the rebate or quirk of the moulding, not from the outer edge of the latter. A haunch could be cut at the outside with advantage.

In certain barred doors in which the glass is beaded rather than puttied in, the rebate is not so deep as the moulding, and this necessitates long and short shoulders. With puttied glass there is no difficulty and the simpler joint shown at B should be used.

Twin tenons, C. When jointing heavy material such as table legs, etc., this two-tenon joint is useful. Where practicable the tenon can be taken right through and wedged. Both tenons and mortises should be marked with the mortise gauge from the face side.

Double tenons, D. For wide stuff this joint is necessary. The number of tenons can be increased to three or four for extra wide stuff. In the latter case it is simpler to work the tenons with the rebate plane rather than the saw. In all cases it is advisable to plough a groove in line with the joint on the mortised piece. This necessitates a continuous haunch running right across the tenons to fill in the groove.

FIG. 5. DOVETAILED JOINTS—THE VARIOUS KINDS.

DOVETAILED JOINTS, Fig. 5

Through-dovetail, A. As the joint shows on both surfaces it is confined generally to concealed work, though there is a growing tendency frankly to expose joints nowadays for their decorative value. For coarse work a slope of about $\frac{5}{8}$ in. in 3 in. is often used (see D), though many craftsmen prefer a lower angle, especially for decorative dovetails. For this it may be $\frac{3}{8}$ in. or $\frac{1}{2}$ in. in 3 in. The usual procedure is to saw the dovetails and mark out the pins from them, placing the dovetailed piece in position and drawing the saw along each kerf in turn. When the pins are cut the saw is held on the waste side of the mark. Some prefer to cut the dovetails in their entirety and mark round with a marking awl. It is a good plan to make a dovetail marker, the sides of which slope at the correct angle. After practice, however, one learns to saw at the right slope without any guide. Decorative dovetails are shown at H.

Lapped dovetail, B. The chief application of this is in carcase work, the top and bottom being lap-dovetailed to the ends. The advantage is that it is invisible from the sides. It is also invariably used for drawer fronts, though these have a special arrangement (see page 102). Other applications are given on pages 71 and 79.

Double-lapped dovetail, C. This is entirely concealed on one surface, and appears only as a thin line of end grain on the other. It is simpler to cut than the mitre dovetail and is largely used for jointing bureau tops to the ends.

Mitre dovetail, E. Since the dovetails are entirely concealed on all surfaces this is a specially neat joint. It is used on the best work for jointing the top to the sides when there is no false top, and for plinths, etc., made in the best way. In this joint the pins must be sawn first and the dovetails marked from them as it is impossible to mark the pins from the dovetails. The mitre of the lap is best worked with the shoulder plane. A special guide-piece with its edge planed at 45 deg. can be cramped at the back to serve as a guide for the plane.

Stopped-slot dovetail, F. For jointing a T stretcher to its end rails this is a handy joint. It is stopped at the top so that the dovetail cannot be seen from above. For a concealed position it could be taken right through.

Barefaced-slot dovetail, G. This is in a similar class to the above, but does not take so long to cut. It is often used for the centre strengthening rails of plinths, etc.

Dovetail angle, D. Measure the required slope along one edge of a square corner and 3 in. along the other. A line joining these points gives the angle. See also note on slope above.

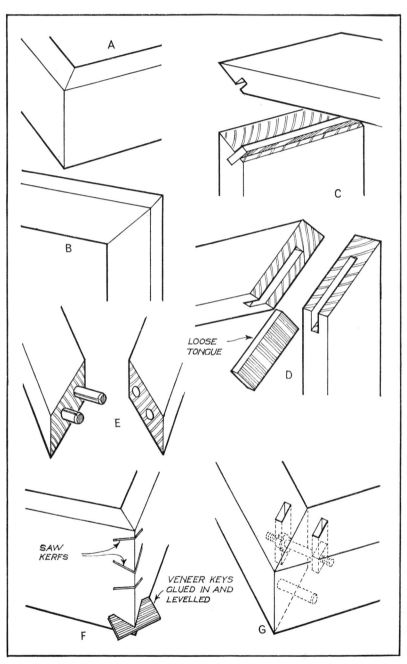

FIG. 6. MITRED JOINTS AND METHODS OF STRENGTHENING THEM.

MITRED JOINTS, Fig. 6

Simple mitre, A and B. This is used for joining pieces in their thickness (A) as for a plinth, or their width (B) as in a frame. The joint is widely used for mouldings of all kinds. The line of the mitre halves the over-all angle. Thus, for the common right angle the mitre is cut at 45 deg.

Tongued mitre, C and D. Both the thickness (C) and width (D) joints are given. Either could be stopped or taken right through.

Dowelled mitre, E. A simple way of strengthening the plain mitre. If their appearance on the outer edges is not an objection, the holes can be bored right through after the mitre has been glued together.

Veneer-keyed mitre, F. Specially useful for boxes, etc. which are to be veneered, and which are not subjected to great strain. Saw cuts are made after the mitre has been glued together. Slips of saw-cut veneer are glued in and levelled later.

Bolted mitre, G. For large mitres such as those on curbs. Handrail bolts are used, the nuts being inserted in slots from beneath. A dowel should also be used to resist any twisting tendency.

Notes on Mitreing

Small mitres are cut on the mitre block, and if a fine saw is used they frequently need no further trimming. If the latter is necessary the mitre shooting-board is used. Details of these tools appear on page 37. For large joints the mitre box is required. Any subsequent trimming should be done on the mitre shooting-block (page 37). Always saw *into* the section of the moulding because, no matter how fine the saw may be, a certain amount of rag is inevitable, and it is better for this to appear on the back of the moulding rather than on the face.

Not all mitres are at 45 deg. The rule is always to halve the over-all angle. Thus, mouldings meeting at 135 deg. would have a mitre angle of $67\frac{1}{2}$ deg. The simplest plan is to make a special kerf on the mitre block for sawing whatever angle is needed. When a mitre is being nailed as well as glued allow the top piece to stand a trifle proud because the tapping with the hammer is bound to cause the joint to slip somewhat. A good plan is to drive the nail through the top piece so that it emerges slightly at the mitre before placing the parts together.

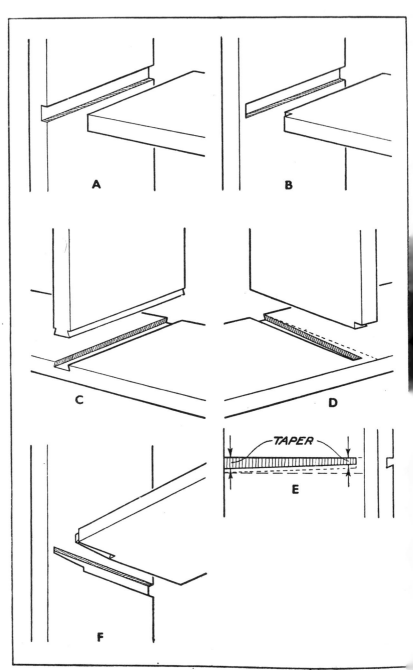

FIG. 7. HOUSED JOINTS USED FOR CARCASE WORK, ETC.

HOUSED JOINTS, Fig. 7

Simple housing, A. Frequently used for loose shelves, this consists of a plain groove to take the shelf. It can also be used for fixed shelves or partitions where there is no liability for the grooved part to bow outwards.

Stopped housing, B. Useful when it is desired to conceal the groove at the front.

Dovetailed housing, C. Stronger than the simple housing in that it resists any outward pull. It can also be stopped as at B.

Barefaced dovetailed housing, D. Simpler to cut than the dovetailed housing. It is an advantage to taper it in its length as it makes fitting simpler. This is shown at E.

Part dovetail housed, F. Easier to cut than either C or D. The dovetail occurs at the front only. Taper the dovetail preferably.

General Notes

Through-grooves can either be worked with a trenching plane, or the sides can be sawn, the waste partly chiselled away, and finished with the router. A stopped groove cannot be trenched. A recess should be chiselled against the stop to allow the end of the saw to emerge. The latter will have to be worked in short strokes. It is then a matter of chiselling away the waste and finishing off with the router. Dovetailed housings must be cut with the saw held at the correct dovetail angle. A piece of wood cut at one end to this angle can be fixed temporarily to the side of the groove to act as a guide for the saw. The dovetail on the shelf can be sawn across and chiselled. The side-rebate plane is useful for any trimming that may be needed.

Mitred shoulder mortise and tenon

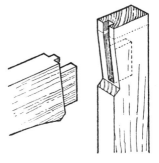

This is used chiefly for door frames and stands in which the top rail has its lower edge curved. When the shoulder is square there is necessarily short grain at the end of the curve, whereas the mitre shown here gives longer grain. There are two ways of making the joint. One is to make the main shoulder slope as shown; the other is to gauge a line parallel with the edge, and cut away the wood. This enables square shoulders to be cut with the mitre at the lower edge.

FIG. 7a. MITRED SHOULDER MORTISE AND TENON.

DOWELLED JOINTS, Fig. 8

Dowelled shaped framework, A. This is preferable to the mortise and tenon as the latter would be liable to snap off (see inset).

Circular frame, B. A strong joint between the segments of a circular frame. The joint is concealed. Note the lugs which enable the frame to be cramped together. They are sawn off after assembling.

Dowelled foot, D. Preferably the dowel would be turned on the foot, but sometimes a loose dowel is necessary. **C** is another application for fixing a lug. If the applied piece is to be carved care must be taken in positioning the dowels so that the carving does not reveal them.

Dowels are also used for strengthening rubbed joints (see page 44).

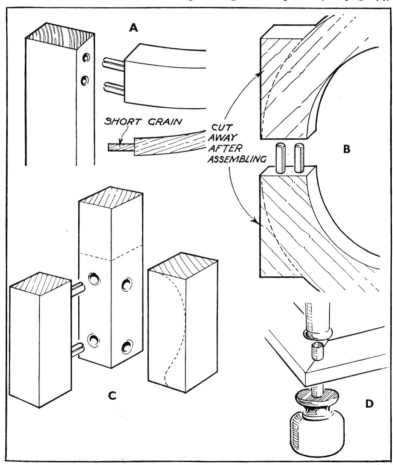

FIG. 8. VARIOUS APPLICATIONS OF DOWELLED JOINTS.

LAPPED, AND TONGUED AND GROOVED JOINTS, Fig. 9

Lapped joint, A. This is handy for joining the corners of light work, but nails are needed to hold the parts in addition to glue.

Double-lapped joint, B. A variation of the above, and probably slightly stronger. Sometimes used for small boxes, etc.

Barefaced tongue and groove, C. An alternative to the lapped joint at A. It has the advantage that nails need not be used. It is suitable only for light work as there is short grain at the groove.

Tongued and grooved joint, D. Frequently used for clamping bureau falls, table tops, etc., though in the best work a series of tenons joined by the tongue is used. Dry stuff must be used as shrinkage may cause a split. The tongue must be no more than a hand-tight fit. If too tight it may cause the sides of the groove to split away.

The joints at E and F are variations of the lapped and grooved joints. They are not strong, and F is suitable for machine work only.

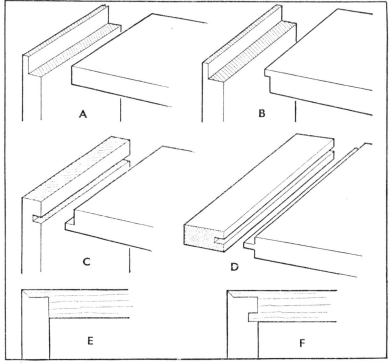

FIG. 9. LAPPED, AND TONGUED AND GROOVED JOINTS.

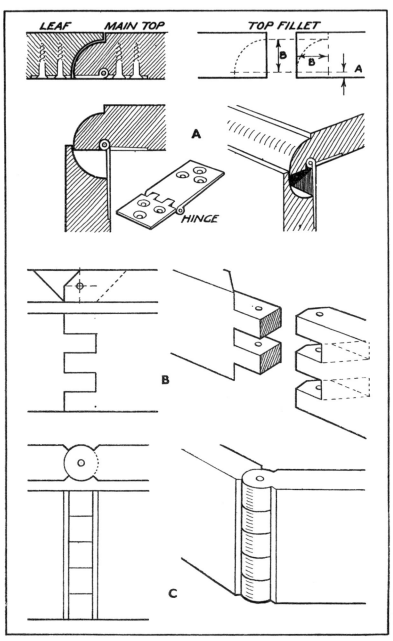

LEAF   MAIN TOP   TOP FILLET

A

HINGE

B

C

FIG. 10. RULE JOINT, FINGER JOINT, AND KNUCKLE JOINT.

MECHANICAL JOINTS, Figs. 10 and 11

Rule joint, A. Fig. 10. Used for flap tables at the hingeing edge. Special hinges, countersunk upon the reverse side so that the knuckle projects into the thickness of the wood, are used. One flap is wider than the other so that it bridges across the gap formed by the hollow of the flap. Set gauge to hinge centre (A) and mark *ends* of main top (not joint edge). Decide thickness of top fillet and gauge in at ends of main top, and on joint edges of top and leaf, gauging from bottom. Distance between two gauge lines gives size (B). Set gauge to this and mark ends, top, and bottom of main top, and bottom of leaf. Intersection gives hinge centre.

Finger joint, B, Fig. 10. This is a simple alternative to the knuckle joint, C. The whole thing can be cut with saw and straight chisel cuts. The bottoms of the notches are cut at 45 deg. enabling the square corners of the moving parts to clear.

Knuckle joint, C, Fig. 10. Swing legs or swing brackets are pivoted with the knuckle joint in the best work. A metal rod forms the pivot. The centre must be set in from the ends by exactly half the thickness of the wood. Mark out circles at top and bottom, work the rounded shape, and mark the knuckles, gauging from the same side in every case. Hold the saw on the waste side so that the parts fit reasonably tightly. Cramp together and bore from each edge.

Rebated fall joint, A, Fig. 11. The advantage is that the fall is flush with the writing top when opened, and when closed there is no gap at the front.

Pivoting bracket, B, Fig. 11. Useful for light tables for supporting a flap. Note how the ends are cut askew to give clearance.

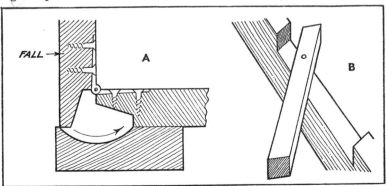

FIG. 11. REBATED FALL JOINT, AND PIVOTED BRACKET.

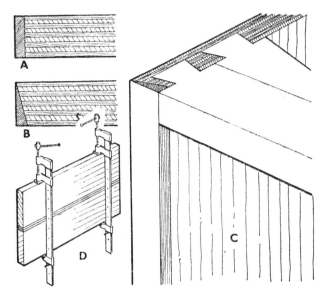

FIG. 12. TWO SIMPLE LIPPINGS FOR PLYWOOD.

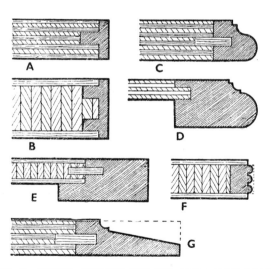

FIG. 13. SPECIAL LIPPINGS FOR PLY AND LAMIN BOARD.

PLYWOOD AND LAMIN-BOARD JOINTS, Figs. 12, 13, and 14

Lippings, Fig. 12. These are needed to conceal the layers at the edges. A shows the simplest form. A thickness shows on both surfaces, but for some work this may not matter. If veneered afterwards it would not show at all. D, Fig. 12, shows how such lippings can be put on two at a time. If the appearance of the lipping on the surface is an objection, the feathered type given at B can be used. It is handy for carcase work, the " point " facing outwards as at C.

A stronger form of lipping is that at A, Fig. 13. If fixed before veneering it is concealed by the veneer ; if afterwards, it acts as a protective edging to the veneer. A similar idea can be followed for thick lamin board as at B. C is for a top with a moulded edging. The moulding is worked after fixing. D gives an appearance of extra thickness. It may be unwise to work a solid tongue around a lamin board top because of the short grain. E, Fig. 13, shows how a loose tongue can be fitted. The rebate increases the gluing surface. F shows how lamin board can have its core grooved away to receive an edging to be moulded. G shows a fielded panel. This would be tongued on as a rectangular piece (see dotted lines), be veneered, and moulded afterwards.

Corner joints, Fig. 14. A simple form of grooved joint is that at A, Fig. 14. As applied to ply or lamin board it has its weakness in that the end piece is liable to snap off along the joint. Rather better is the lapped joint at B. This needs to be nailed as well as glued, and care has to be taken to avoid splitting down the layers. Used for lamin board, as at C, it is satisfactory in every way.

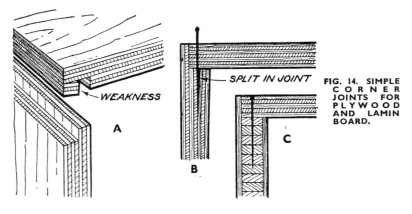

WEAKNESS

A

SPLIT IN JOINT

B

C

FIG. 14. SIMPLE CORNER JOINTS FOR PLYWOOD AND LAMIN BOARD.

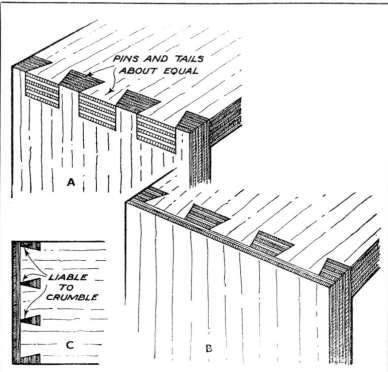

FIG. 15. DOVETAIL JOINTS USED FOR PLYWOOD.
A is the through-dovetail ; B, lapped dovetail ; C, drawer dovetails.

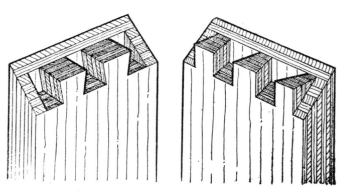

FIG. 16. SECRET-MITRED DOVETAIL APPLIED TO PLYWOOD.

PLYWOOD AND LAMIN-BOARD JOINTS, Figs. 15, 16, and 17

Dovetails. When practicable the simple through-dovetail at A, Fig. 15, is the strongest joint for plywood. The pins and tails should be of about equal size. The lapped dovetail at B is also sound and has the advantage of being concealed at one side. Note that very narrow pins such as those used for drawers are not practicable (C), the short grain being liable to crumble. For work in which the joint must be hidden on both surfaces either the double-lapped dovetail or the mitre dovetail must be used (Fig. 16). This is the strongest form of corner joint for plywood in which both the edge layers and the joint itself are concealed.

The dovetail can be applied to lamin board, but the direction of the grain should be that in Fig. 17. In this way the main strength comes from the core.

The general procedure for dovetailing ply and lamin board is similar to that for solid wood, but care should be taken not to cut in too deeply with the cutting gauge as this may go right through the outer layer of ply and sever it, rendering the end piece liable to chip off. The assembling must also be done cautiously to avoid separating the plies. The corners of the top layer in particular are liable to chip out. Always place a piece of waste wood over the joint and strike this with the hammer (this, of course, should be done in all dovetailed work).

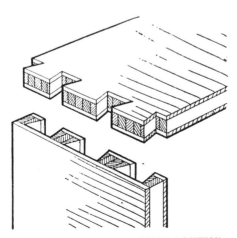

FIG. 17. LAMIN-BOARD LAPPED DOVETAIL.

PLYWOOD AND LAMIN-BOARD JOINTS

Tongues. If the dovetail is not suitable the tongued joint in Fig. 18 is a strong alternative. The groove is not cut right through, consisting instead of a series of short grooves separated by uncut wood. The latter prevents the edge from crumbling.

Corner blocks. The glued and screwed corner block, Fig. 18, is useful for angles. Still stronger is the corner bracket, Fig. 18, in which two pieces of solid wood are dovetailed together and glued and screwed in the angle. Ends of both tails and pins should be slightly bare so that they do not protrude if the wood shrinks. These joints can generally be used when there is a frieze at the top of a carcase to conceal the block or bracket. The lap in both joints can either be left square or mitred. It is an advantage to let the lap line up with one of the plywood joints.

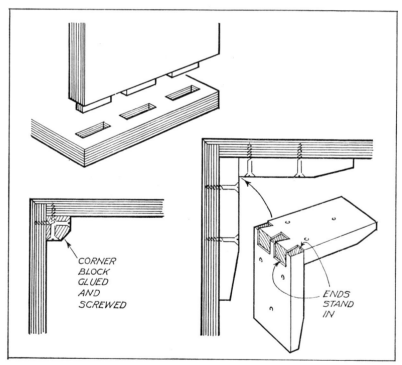

FIG. 18. STRONG CORNER JOINT. SCREWED CORNER BLOCK. DOVETAILED CORNER BRACKET GLUED AND SCREWED.

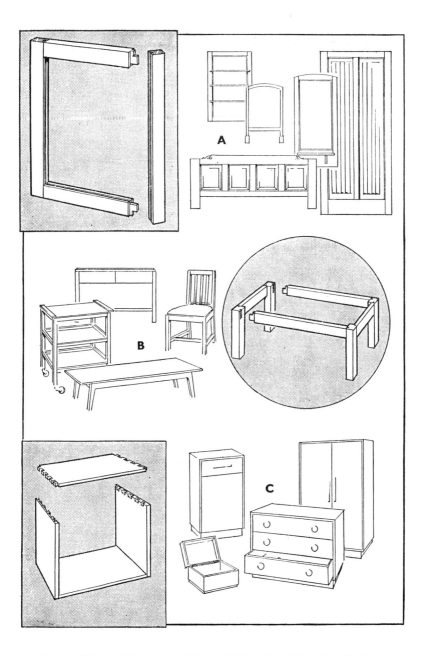

FIG. I. MAIN SYSTEMS OF CONSTRUCTION AND THEIR APPLICATIONS
A is framed construction; B stool construction, and C box construction.

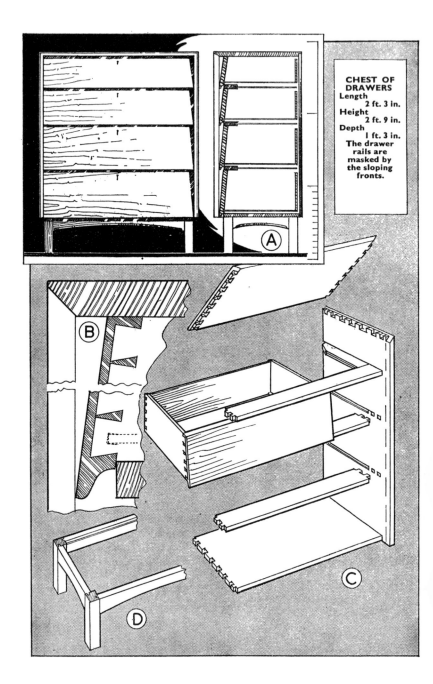

CHEST OF DRAWERS
Length
2 ft. 3 in.
Height
2 ft. 9 in.
Depth
1 ft. 3 in.
The drawer rails are masked by the sloping fronts.

PART I

WHATEVER the furniture you make you will invariably use one of three forms of construction, or a combination of them ; the frame, stool, and box.   They form the basis of nearly all cabinet construction, and one or more of them can generally be adapted to suit any design.   An exception occurs sometimes in shaped work which may call for special methods.

Systems of construction.   The three are shown in Fig. 1. It is at once clear that the frame can be elaborated into a door or piece of panelling by the addition of further rails ; the stool could become the framework of a sideboard or table ; and the box might develop into the carcase of a chest of drawers or cupboard. All three systems have been largely evolved to meet the two chief characteristics of wood ; its greater strength along than across the grain, and its liability to shrink in its width.   It is because plywood and laminated board are free from these weaknesses that modern construction using these materials is different from the old.

Frame construction.   Typical examples of the application of this are mirror frames, panelling, table tops (when framed), screens, backs, and so on.   Doors obviously come under the same heading, but these form so wide a subject that they are dealt with separately.

The point about the method is that it overcomes the bad effects of shrinkage in timber and at the same time provides strength in both length and width.   Glance at Fig. 2.   The panel, which might fit in either a groove or rebate, is entirely free to shrink or swell without affecting the framework (it is never glued).   Strength is ensured by the framework, the grain of which runs in its length along both width and height, so giving rigidity in both directions.   Either mortised and tenoned or mitred joints are used at the corners.   The last named are not so strong and come in for lighter work as a rule.

Stool construction.   In a sense this may be regarded as four frames put together to form a rectangle in plan, except that there is

The systems shown on the opposite page are for solid wood, and their uses are fairly obvious. The use of plywood has introduced a new method in which work may be bent and laminated to the desired shape, or may be moulded or compressed.   This, however, generally involves the use of special presses, and scarcely comes within the scope of this book.

69

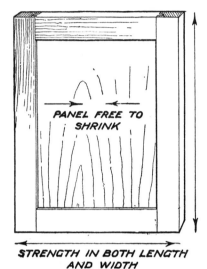

PANEL FREE TO SHRINK

STRENGTH IN BOTH LENGTH AND WIDTH

FIG. 2. HOW A FRAMEWORK PROVIDES STRENGTH YET ALLOWS FOR SHRINKAGE.

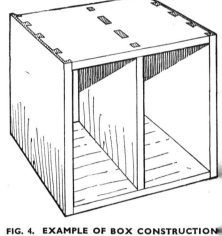

FIG. 4. EXAMPLE OF BOX CONSTRUCTION

It is desirable to arrange the grain so that the whole shrinks together, thus avoiding splitting.

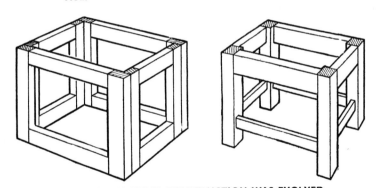

FIG. 3. HOW STOOL CONSTRUCTION WAS EVOLVED.

The method consists virtually of four frames joined together as shown to the left. The same result is achieved by using solid legs (right).

usually only one post or leg at each corner (see Fig. 3). Here again the shrinkage problem is overcome as in the case of the frame, and strength is provided in all directions. Items made under the system include tables, chairs, stands, and the framework of some cabinets. A point to remember when using the method is that, since wood does not shrink in its length, the resulting carcase will not shrink. Consequently any solid wood fitted across it (such as a top) must not be

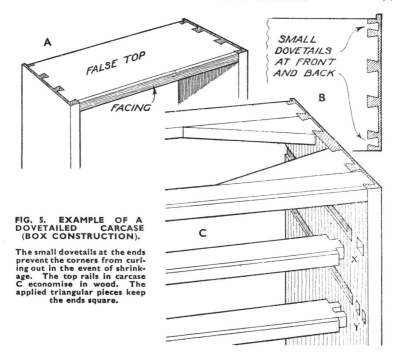

SMALL
DOVETAILS
AT FRONT
AND BACK

FALSE TOP

FACING

A

B

C

X

Y

FIG. 5. EXAMPLE OF A DOVETAILED CARCASE (BOX CONSTRUCTION).

The small dovetails at the ends prevent the corners from curling out in the event of shrinkage. The top rails in carcase C economise in wood. The applied triangular pieces keep the ends square.

secured rigidly.   Otherwise it is liable to split in the event of shrinkage.

Box construction.   This is used for all box-like carcases which are made from solid wood as distinct from panelled frames.   The shrinkage difficulty does not exist because the whole thing shrinks equally as shown in Fig. 4.   Chests of drawers, sideboards, cupboards, and any other items built out of solid wood without framing come under the heading.   It should be noted that it is dangerous to mix ply or lamin board with solid wood for a carcase of any great depth, because, whereas the one shrinks, the other will not, and this may cause splitting.

CARCASES

Dovetailed carcases.   The most useful joint for this is the lapped dovetail, the advantage being that it is entirely concealed at the sides.   It is applied to a bookcase at A, Fig. 5.   Assuming that a top proper is to be fixed above, the false top can be in a cheaper softwood with a facing of hardwood at the front.   For a much deeper carcase such as would be needed for a chest of drawers an economy can be effected at the top by using rails with angle brackets as at C, Fig. 5.   The bottom would have to run to the full width, of course, and it is advisable to cut small dovetails at front and back as at B to prevent any tendency for the corners to curl away.

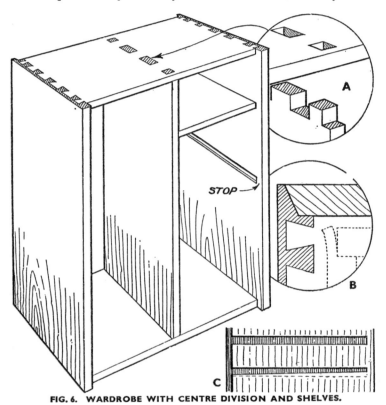

STOP →

FIG. 6. WARDROBE WITH CENTRE DIVISION AND SHELVES.

The through tenoned joint between division and top and bottom is given at A. Sloping rebate for back to minimise tendency to curl is shown at B. Plain housing and dovetailed housing are shown at C.

Drawer rails are stub-tenoned into the ends as at X and Y.   The double tenon Y is better in every way.   Apart from being stronger the rail is bound to fit square, whereas the single tenon X may easily twist over at an angle.

Wardrobes have frequently to be made with inner partitions, and the strongest joint is the through tenon at A, Fig. 6.   Its strength can be still further increased by wedging from above.

Fixed shelves can be plain-housed or (preferably) dovetail-housed, C. In both cases a stop is allowed at the front so that the joint is concealed.   Note that the dovetail at C is tapered, this being much easier to fit than the parallel form and is just as strong.   The point is that it is quite loose until pushed practically home.   It is thus easy

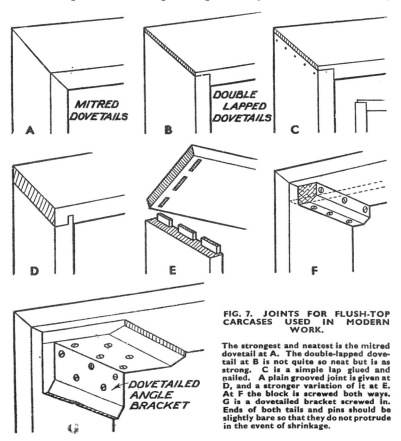

FIG. 7.   JOINTS FOR FLUSH-TOP CARCASES   USED   IN   MODERN WORK.

The strongest and neatest is the mitred dovetail at A. The double-lapped dovetail at B is not quite so neat but is as strong.   C is a simple lap glued and nailed. A stronger variation of it at E. At F the block is screwed both ways. G is a dovetailed bracket screwed in. Ends of both tails and pins should be slightly bare so that they do not protrude in the event of shrinkage.

to detect where it may be tight.   One further point worth noting in Fig. 6 is that the rebate for the back is at an angle (B).   If it were cut square the narrow piece left might curl outwards, and in any case would be weak and liable to break off.   It does not matter when the back is comparatively thin.

Modern furniture.   The modern tendency to eliminate mouldings and overhangs means that the top proper has to form part of the construction, and not be a merely ornamental part screwed on from beneath. In other words there cannot be a false top. Assuming that the dovetails must not be visible, either the double-lapped dovetail or the mitre dovetail forms the best joint. These are illustrated on page 52.

Simpler alternatives are given in Fig. 7. C is a simple lapped joint which is quite strong, but must be nailed. Nails are not necessary for D, but its strength is rather limited because of the short grain at the side of the groove. The best plan is to keep the latter as narrow as possible because this increases the width of the wood at the side.

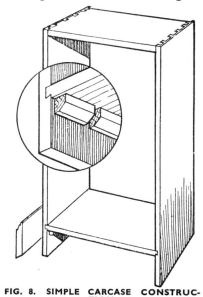

FIG. 8. SIMPLE CARCASE CONSTRUCTION.

Here the plinth is made in one with the main carcase. If the latter is deep the sides of the plinth should be glued at the front only.

A stronger joint, but one which takes considerably longer to cut, is that at E. Here the weakness of the short grain is helped by the uncut " bridges " between the grooves. It means that the grooves have to be chopped with the chisel instead of being ploughed.

When there is no objection to inner corner pieces being used the device at G offers a useful joint. Dovetailed corner brackets are made up and these are screwed inside the corners. These provide the real strength, the corners of the ends and top being either mitred as shown or lapped. A variation of the same idea is given at F.

The bottom is usually fixed similarly to the top in work having a separate plinth, but it is sometimes desirable to make the plinth in one with the main carcase, and in this case the bottom can generally be dovetail-housed into the ends as in Fig. 8. Glue blocks are rubbed into the angle beneath. If a plain-housed joint is used nails should be driven in at the outside, these being dovetailed to give maximum strength. They will be concealed by the plinth to be applied later.

It sometimes happens that legs or posts have to be incorporated with the ends, and these can be either tongued-and-grooved as in

Fig. 9, or dowelled as inset at A.   Top rails with their angle brackets are dovetailed into both leg and end panel as shown, thereby locking the two together.   The panels are glued to the legs before the rails are dovetailed in.   Note how the rail ends have to be cut to fit round the legs.   Since the legs necessarily extend downwards the

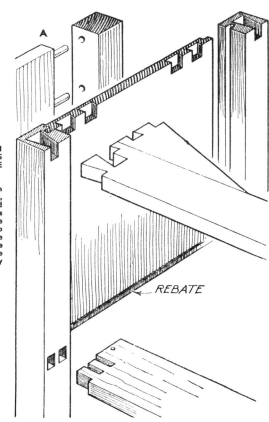

A

FIG. 9. CONSTRUCTION WHEN POSTS OR LEGS ARE IN ONE WITH THE CARCASE.

This method is often used in sideboards, dressing tables, and so on.   A solid top could be fitted but separate rails are more economical.   The triangular pieces serve to hold the job square.   Note the double tenons in the drawer rail.   These are much more satisfactory than a single large tenon.

REBATE

lower rails cannot be dovetailed, but are tenoned as shown.   A rebate is generally worked at the bottom edge of the rail to hold a bottom, and the rail can fit in this and be screwed.

Should the grain of the ends run from back to front it would not be practicable to fit a wide solid top because it would be liable to split in the event of shrinkage, owing to the movement being opposed by the ends.   The better plan would be to fit two rails with corner brackets as in Fig. 9, or fit three rails as in Fig. 10.   Alternatively,

FIG. 10. ARRANGEMENT WHEN GRAIN OF ENDS RUNS FROM FRONT TO BACK.

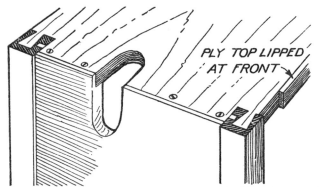

PLY TOP LIPPED AT FRONT

FIG. 11. ALTERNATIVE TO FIG. 10, USING PLY OR LAMIN BOARD FOR TOP.

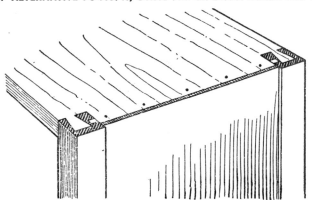

FIG. 12. SOLID TOP DOVETAILED TO POSTS AND FITTING IN REBATE IN ENDS.

In all three examples the grooves are taken right through for simplicity in working. The tongues in Figs. 11 and 12 are necessarily cut away when the top rebates of the ends are worked, but these can be filled in afterwards.

a thick ply top could be dovetailed into the legs and screwed in a rebate in the ends (see Fig. 11). The through-rebate in the ends has the advantage that it can be worked with the rebate plane.

A similar idea can be carried out in solid wood providing the grain of the end panels is upright. The top is dovetailed to the logs and glued and nailed in a rebate in the end panel as in Fig. 12.

Framed carcases. These are frequently used for oak work made in the traditional manner, and are put together largely with

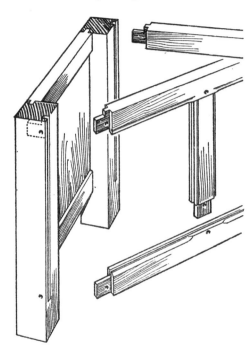

FIG. 13. FRAMED OAK CAR-CASE OF CHEST TYPE.

The strength is provided by the various rails and uprights. Panels are virtually fillings. They fit in grooves, and, being dry, they are free to shrink along their grooves. Danger of splitting is thus eliminated.

mortise and tenon joints. A typical example is the simple chest which is virtually four pieces of panelling assembled to form the sides, except that the legs are common to the adjoining sides. Fig. 13 shows how the parts fit together. The rails are through-grooved, but the leg grooves must be stopped at the bottom rails. It is of course necessary to set in the tenons by the depth of the grooves, and allow haunches on the top rails to fill in the ends of the grooves. The tenons can be made their maximum length by allowing the mortises to meet in the thickness of the legs, cutting the tenon ends at an angle.

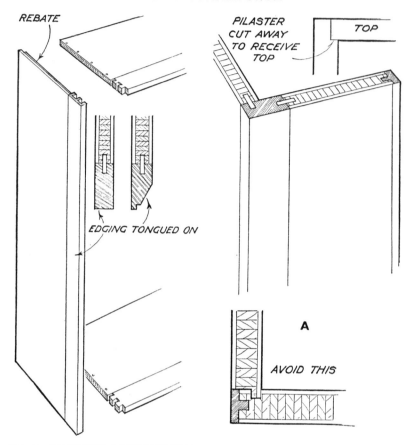

REBATE

PILASTER
CUT AWAY
TO RECEIVE
TOP

TOP

EDGING TONGUED ON

A

AVOID THIS

FIG. 14. WARDROBE CONSTRUCTION.

The ends are of blockboard with front edging of solid wood.

FIG. 15. WIDE PILASTERS.

Here again edged blockboard is used. Note bad construction (A) where grooves nearly sever the corner.

Wardrobe carcases are usually of veneered blockboard or multi-ply, and construction can be as in Fig. 14, the edges being lipped and the top and bottom part-dovetailed and part rebated and screwed. When there are pilasters construction can follow Fig. 15. Note that the wide lipping of the pilaster masks the edge of the end. Be careful to avoid the trap (A), where the two grooves practically meet, leaving an isolated corner which is nearly severed. If possible, the pilaster should be shallow rebated to receive the top, and the latter fixed by pocket screwing or dowelling.

CORNER CABINETS

Carcases. In the best way the backs of corner carcases are framed together, the advantage being that they are not liable to shrink. Of course, if ply or blockboard is used there is no difficulty. Fig. 16 shows a plan of such a carcase. Note that pilasters are

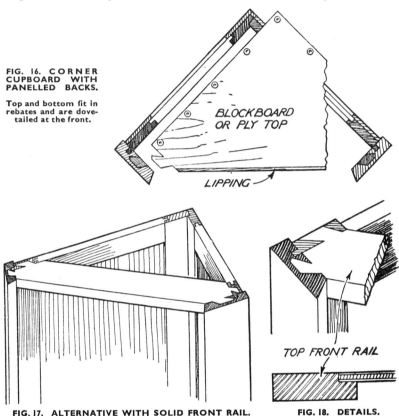

FIG. 16. CORNER CUPBOARD WITH PANELLED BACKS.

Top and bottom fit in rebates and are dove-tailed at the front.

BLOCKBOARD OR PLY TOP

LIPPING

TOP FRONT RAIL

FIG. 17. ALTERNATIVE WITH SOLID FRONT RAIL.   **FIG. 18. DETAILS.**

The front rail can be rebated at the back so that a plywood filling can be added as shown in Fig. 18.

invariably introduced, partly to give increased rigidity, and because they help the design. It is always advisable to allow them to project a trifle at the sides towards the wall because then, if the wall is not perfectly square, there will not be a gap showing at the sides. In the best work they are rebated or tongued to the backs, and the top and bottom are dovetailed in.

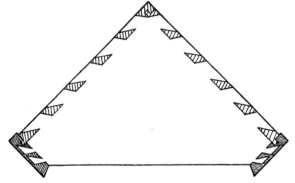

FIG. 19. SOLID WOOD CONSTRUCTION FOR CORNER CABINET.

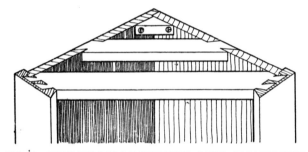

FIG. 20. SEPARATE RAILS DOVETAILED, SOLID CARCASE ENDS.

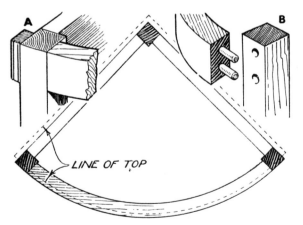

FIG. 21. STAND FOR BOW FRONT CORNER CABINET.

It will be seen from Fig. 16 that the top is screwed into rebates in the back frames and is dovetailed to the pilasters. Such a top should be of ply or blockboard if possible because it will not shrink against the rigid end frames. If solid wood is used make sure that it is dry. An alternative is to have a solid front rail dovetailed in with a ply filling at the back, fitting in a rebate in the rail as in Fig. 17. Assuming that the ply is thinner than the rail the end frames will have to be cut down to finish level with the rebate (see Fig. 18).

Yet another construction is given in Fig. 19 in which solid wood can be used throughout if desired. Note that the top and bottom

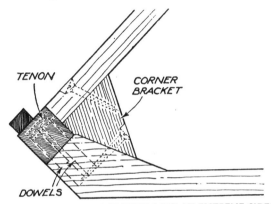

TENON   CORNER BRACKET

DOWELS

FIG. 22. ARRANGEMENT WITH LEGS AT EXTREME SIDES.

Dowels are better than tenons owing to short grain.

are both dovetailed. There is no liability to split because the whole thing can shrink together. The same thing applies to Fig. 20 in which separate rails and a back block are used. Here it is assumed that a top proper is to be fitted over the whole.

Corner stands, etc. Small corner tables or stands for corner cupboards have sometimes to be made, and the construction depends largely upon the leg positions. When the stand is bow-fronted the side rails are tenoned into back and front legs. As the front rail would necessarily show short grain if tenoned it is generally more satisfactory to dowel as in Fig. 21. Since most rooms are fitted with a skirting it is invariably necessary to arrange for the cupboard to project at the sides of the stand. In the case of a table small blocks are screwed on outside and the top kept level with this. The top thus reaches right through to the walls although the legs clear the skirting.

If the cabinet above is straight at the front and the legs have to be at the extreme sides, the front rail can be shaped in plan as shown in Fig. 22 and be dowelled in. Strengthening angle blocks can be added inside. Note the filling blocks added at the outsides of the legs opposite the rails.

A more satisfactory arrangement is to place the legs beneath the front corners as in Fig. 23. The advantage is that, being more forward, they are better able to resist any tendency for the cabinet to

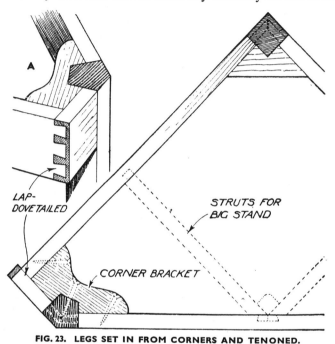

A

LAP-
DOVETAILED

STRUTS FOR
BIG STAND

CORNER BRACKET

FIG. 23. LEGS SET IN FROM CORNERS AND TENONED.
They give the cabinet greater stability as they reach to the extreme front.

fall forward. The whole thing can be tenoned, the short end rails being dovetailed to the back rails and strengthened with glued blocks.

TABLE AND STAND FRAMES

By far the commonest joint in table framings is the mortise and tenon as shown in Fig. 24. The inset sketches (E and F) show how the mortises meet in the thickness of the leg, so allowing the tenons to be the maximum length. They can be either cut at an angle (E) or be cut back as at F. In most cases the simple tenon at A can be arranged, but a rather better arrangement is to allow a haunch as at

B as this resists any twisting tendency of the top of the rail where it is wholly unsupported as in A. C shows an alternative haunch which is entirely concealed. It is also rather stronger in that the leg is not cut away so much.

The joint used for the stretcher rail depends upon the thickness. If similar to the top rails it would be jointed similarly, but if thin it

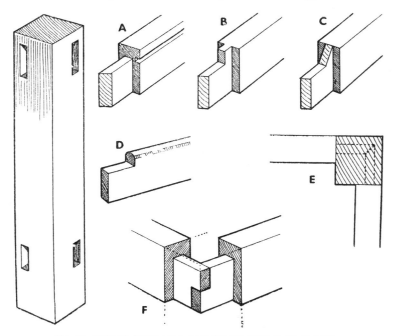

FIG. 24. JOINTS USED FOR FRAMED-UP TABLE OR STAND.

A. Simple tenon. **B.** Tenon with haunch. **C.** Secret haunch. **D.** Barefaced tenon for stretcher. **E.** Tenons cut at angle to meet in thickness of leg. **F.** Alternative halving.

could have the bare-faced tenon at D. The top shoulder is advisable because it gives a definite length, and enables the top corners to be rounded or moulded if required.

When a drawer has to be fitted the rails generally have to lie flat, and the joints shown in Fig. 25 can be used. The double dovetail has the effect of binding the rail to the leg. Note that it is an advantage to keep the ends of all dovetails level. The lower rail is double-tenoned in and is cut around the leg.

When a centre leg is introduced a convenient form of joint is the bridle joint in Fig. 28. Here the top rail runs right through in a

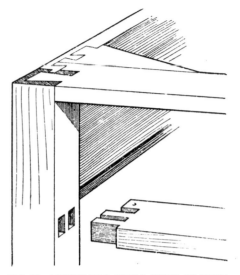

FIG. 25. JOINTS FOR TABLE WITH DRAWER RAIL TENONED IN.

FIG. 26. CABRIOLE LEG WITH RAILS TENONED IN.

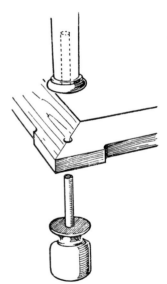

FIG. 27. FIXING STRETCHER BETWEEN TURNED LEG AND FOOT.

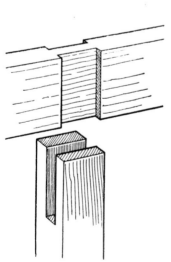

FIG. 28. BRIDLE JOINT USEFUL FOR CENTRE LEG.

single length, the leg fitting into it.   Lower rails, drawer rails for instance, would be tenoned in.

Cabriole legs present a rather special problem.   They are usually fitted with ear pieces at the top, just below the square, and these, whilst contributing to the strength, do not form the main fixing. The latter is in the top square which is mortised to take the tenons of the rails as in Fig. 26.   By driving in screws through the ear pieces considerable extra solidity is attained. These can be put in after the joint has been glued and has set.

In certain period pieces, notably the William and Mary style, flat stretchers are frequently used as in Fig. 27.   The best plan is to make up the stretcher as a complete framework, using either tongued or mortise and tenon joints according to the design.   Sometimes it is more convenient to halve the corners.   Holes are bored through this and into the bottom ends of the legs, and turned feet with dowels are glued in right through the stretcher.

When a table top of solid wood is fitted it should not be rigidly fixed with screws because its shrinkage will be opposed by the rails of the frame.   The simplest fixing is given in Fig. 29.   At the front where the same overhang (or flush finish) is to be maintained screws can be driven in through the rail.   These can be either driven straight through a flat rail, or inserted in pockets of an upright rail as at A.   At sides and back buttons are used.   These are provided with tongues which fit in grooves worked along side and back rails, the tongues being so arranged that there is a slight gap at the top. Thus when screws are driven into the top the latter is pulled hard down on to the rails, yet is free to slide forward if shrinkage occurs.

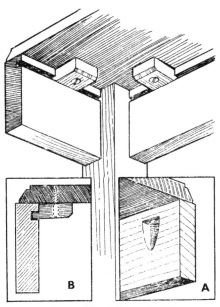

FIG. 29. TABLE TOP FIXING.

The front is pocket-screwed as at A. At sides and back buttons which fit into grooves are used (B). This allows for shrinkage. If ply or lamin board is used it can be plain screwed from beneath.

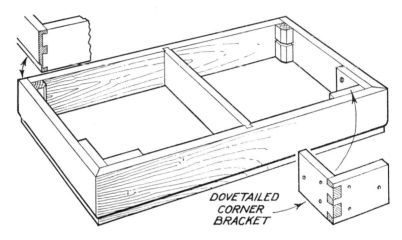

FIG. 30. PLINTH WITH MITRED CORNERS STRENGTHENED WITH BRACKETS,

DOVETAILED
CORNER
BRACKET

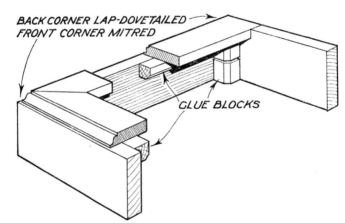

BACK CORNER LAP-DOVETAILED
FRONT CORNER MITRED

GLUE BLOCKS

FIG. 31. MITRED PLINTH WITH MITRED MOULDING PLANTED ON TOP.

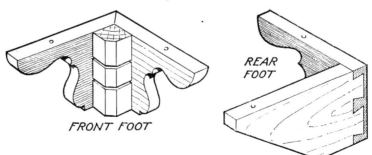

REAR
FOOT

FRONT FOOT

FIG. 32. CONSTRUCTION OF BRACKET FEET, FRONT AND REAR.

PLINTHS

Most plinths to-day are recessed, and in the best construction they should be made up as a separate unit. An example is given in Fig. 30. For maximum strength the front corners should be mitre-dovetailed, but a reliable alternative is to plain-mitre them and screw in through-dovetailed corner brackets as shown. Ends of pins and tails should be slightly short. For cheaper work a large glue block is rubbed in. If the plinth is deep two separate blocks should be used. A centre cross-rail is desirable for a job of any size and this can be slot-dovetailed.

An older form of projecting plinth is given in Fig. 31. The main sides are put together as in the previous example, but the moulding is planted on top, being mitred at the front. Glue blocks are rubbed in the angle beneath.

Bracket feet. In a similar class is the bracket foot used largely on antique furniture. At the front the parts are mitred together and strengthened with glue blocks. Lapped dovetails are used for the back feet. Both are fixed by gluing and screwing, glue blocks being rubbed in the corners afterwards. Fig. 32 shows the idea.

CORNICES

In much modern work these are frequently entirely omitted or appear in reduced form only. This means that a cornice may be little more than a length of battening fixed to the carcase top. You

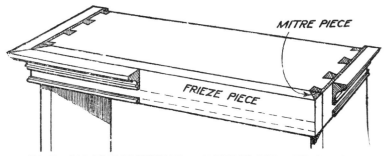

FIG. 33. OLD TIME CORNICE WITH FRIEZE IN ONE WITH CARCASE.
The frieze is planted along the face with mitre pieces at the ends.

still require to know the proper way to make it, however, because a lot of conventional furniture is still made.

In cheaper classes of work a cornice frequently is made as part of the carcase, but this is not really satisfactory. Glance at Fig. 33 which shows a cabinet top made in this way. A frieze is fixed along the front, and, to conceal the end grain at its ends, small mitre pieces

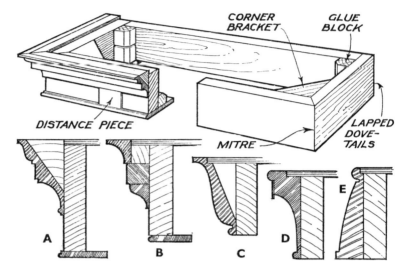

FIG. 34. CORNICE AND FRIEZE MADE UP AS A SEPARATE UNIT.

In the best work the front corners are mitre-dovetailed. The moulding may be backed with softwood (A), built up in layers (B), pitched as at (C), or in the solid (D) and (E).

are fitted as shown.   The cornice and frieze mouldings are mitred and glued round.   The weakness is that the grain of the moulding runs across the ends, and, in the event of the latter shrinking, a split may be caused.   It is satisfactory for narrow carcases.

Loose cornices.   The loose cornice is a much better method. It is shown in Fig. 34, from which it will be seen that the sides are lap-dovetailed to the back and mitred at the front.   Glue blocks and corner brackets are added at the inner corners as shown.   The frieze moulding is mitred round beneath and projects inwards so that it reaches well over the top of the main carcase.   At the top the cornice moulding is fixed, the usual plan being to allow it to

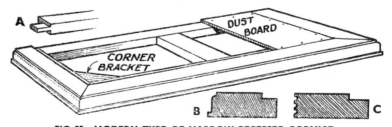

FIG. 35. MODERN TYPE OF NARROW RECESSED CORNICE.

The front mitres may be dowelled to strengthen them, though it is not essential as the cornice takes no great strain.

stand up slightly so that a dustboard can be fixed down flush.   When fixing it a distance piece can be used to ensure the frieze being the same width all round.   (See illustration.)

Mouldings are frequently in the form of a facing with a softwood backing as at A, but sometimes it is an advantage to build up a wide moulding in sections as at B, Fig. 34.   A cheaper alternative is the pitched cornice at C.   It is mitred round and fixed with glue and fine pins.   Specially prepared glue blocks are rubbed in all round to give additional strength.   D and E often have decorative veneers applied.

Fig. 35 shows a more modern form of cornice.   The moulding is mitred at the front and large corner brackets are screwed in to give strength.   It is rebated at the top for a dustboard.   Finishing level with this rebate is the back rail which can be tenoned or dovetailed to the moulding.   If the carcase is extra long a middle cross-rail is desirable.   The mitres of an extra wide moulding can be tongued or dowelled.

BACKS

The simplest form of back is a sheet of plywood, chipboard, or (for a light job) hardboard.   It can be of any thickness from $\frac{1}{8}$ in. upwards, according to the size of the cabinet; but remember that a

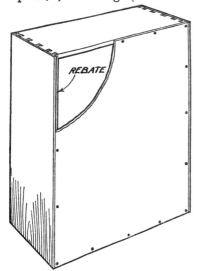

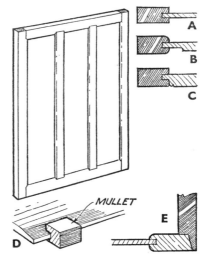

FIG. 36.   SIMPLE PLYWOOD BACK.
The plywood is screwed in the rebates of the ends. Chipboard can also be used.

FIG. 37.   FRAMED AND PANELLED BACK.
A, B, and C are alternative sections.   That at B would require mitres to allow for the rounded corners.   D shows panel tested for thickness when solid wood is used.   E has sloping rebate for back.

back is not just a mere filling and nothing more. The cabinet depends upon it for quite a lot of its rigidity. It must therefore be of reasonable thickness to prevent racking. Furthermore, its weight

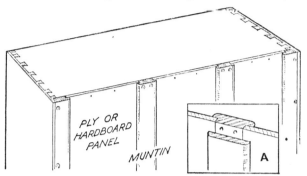

FIG. 38. SIMPLE FORM OF MUNTIN BACK.
This was widely used as a cheap alternative to the panelled back before plywood became popular, but is still sometimes used when ply or hardboard are substituted.

is of definite value, especially pieces which have large doors which are liable to overbalance the cupboard when opened. Fig. 36 shows how such a back generally fits in rebates worked in the ends. Note how the top and bottom are flush with the rebate. Screws are used for fixing, except for small jobs for which nails can be used.

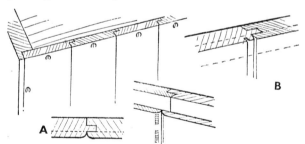

FIG. 39. BACK OF TONGUED-AND-GROOVED BOARDS.
This was largely used on old-time dressers. It is advisable to cut shallow rebates as shown by the dotted lines as this helps to prevent side racking.

A muntin back has the advantage of simplicity. It consists of a series of grooved uprights or muntins screwed to the top and bottom with panels between. Fig. 38 shows the idea. Note how the muntins are cut back as far as the groove so that the panels will be flush. If solid wood is used for the panels, the nails should be inserted near the centre only, not at the sides. The panels will then be free to pull out of their grooves in the event of shrinkage and so not be liable to split. To-day, however, plywood or hardboard is generally used.

An alternative occasionally used is the solid wood tongued-and-grooved back in Fig. 39. Either V or beaded joints should be used so that any opening due to shrinkage is not noticeable. Note that the rebate at top and bottom are most desirable as it helps to resist side racking once the centre screw is inserted.

The most satisfactory back in that it has the greatest rigidity and is free from shrinkage troubles is the panelled type in Fig. 37. The whole thing is put together with mortise and tenon joints, the panels fitting in grooves. Normally the panels are as at A, B, or C, the groove width being arranged to suit. Incidentally, if solid panels are used you can use a mullet for testing the fit as at D.

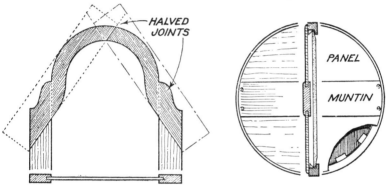

FIG. 40. SHAPED MIRROR BACK.   FIG. 41. CIRCULAR MIRROR BACK.
A simple alternative for either is a sheet of plywood or hardboard.

This mullet is simply an offcut of the rail stuff worked with the same size of groove.

When a back has to present a flush appearance inside, thicker panels are used, their edges being tongued-in as at C.

A note applying to all solid wood backs is that, if the job is to be stained, the panel edges or tongues must be stained before fixing. Otherwise, if a panel pulls out of its groove it will show a line of bare wood.

The panelled back as applied to the backing of a shaped mirror is given in Fig. 40. The three top joints are halved, the shape being cut after assembling. A groove is spindle moulded afterwards to receive the panel. For a circular or oval mirror frame the muntin back in Fig. 41 is satisfactory, though a sheet of ply would be the best back for either this or Fig. 40.

C.M.F.B.—7

PART II

DOOR MAKING

DOORS can be divided conveniently into two groups ; panelled and flush. The former are always framed up ; the latter may be framed, but are more usually made of lamin board or plywood.

PANELLED DOORS

These consist of a framework which provides the main strength, and a centre panel. It is upon the way that the panel fits that the

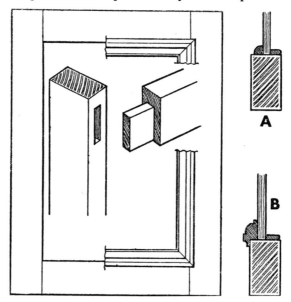

FIG. I. PANELLED DOOR WITH APPLIED MOULDING.
The moulding forms the rebate, and can be either plain as at A,
or of the bolection type (B). The tenon should preferably be haunched.

construction largely depends. It may fit in a rebate worked in the rails or formed by an applied moulding, or it may fit in a groove.

Applied moulding framework. In many ways this is the simplest form of door. The simplicity lies in the fact that the framework is square-edged and there are no complications in the joint. The moulding can be either a simple thumb or hollow section as at A, Fig. 1, or it can be of the bolection type at B—that is, it is rebated and fits over the edge. In both, the panel is held by a bead mitred and pinned round at the back.

Moulded and rebated framework. The most satisfactory

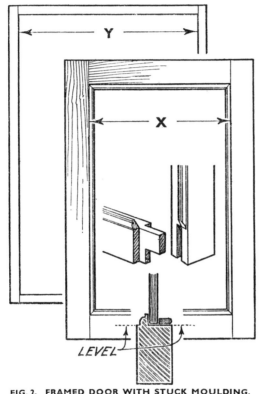

FIG. 2. FRAMED DOOR WITH STUCK MOULDING.
The moulding is worked in the solid and is mitred. Note that
the rebate and moulding quirk are level.

form of moulded door is when the moulding is " stuck " or worked in the solid. It is probably the most widely used construction in cabinet work. As shown in Fig. 2, the quirk of the moulding is level with the rebate, and the moulding is cut away locally at the mortise and is mitred. The mitre template should be used for the mitreing (page 37). A point to note is that the shoulder length of the rails is taken from the moulding or rebate as shown at X, Fig. 2.

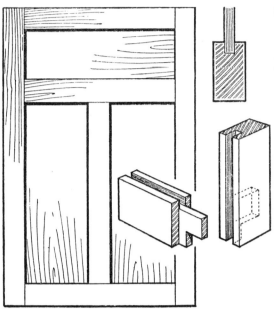

FIG. 3. FRAMED DOOR WITH   GROOVED-IN PANELS.

Note that the haunch fills in the end of the groove which   necessarily   runs right through at the joint.

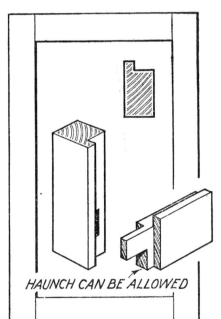

FIG. 4. DOOR WITH REBATED-IN PANEL.

The panel can be added after the framework has been put together. The rebates necessitate the tenon having long and short shoulders.

HAUNCH CAN BE ALLOWED

Grooved-in panel. When there is no objection to the panel being assembled in its framework before polishing the grooved-in construction is followed (Fig. 3). It is seldom used in work to be highly french polished because of the difficulty of reaching into the corners with the rubber, but is successful for the waxed finish. If french polish is to be used it is advisable at least to body-up the panel before assembling in its framework. In any case the edges should be stained first.

The framework edges can be chamfered if preferred. In the rails these can be run right through except where muntin mortises occur, but in the stiles they must be stopped short of the mortises.

Rebated framework. When the edges are to remain square and it is desired to add the panel after assembling the rebated framework is used as in Fig. 4. The only point about it to remember is that the long-and-short shouldered tenon is needed (see page 48). It is handy for mirror frames, cloth-panelled screens, and so on.

Making a panelled door. Prepare the rail and stile material and mark them directly from the job itself. Assuming that the door is to be of the rebated kind, Fig. 5, gauge in on all members both the width and depth of the rebate. Offer the stile against the cupboard and mark with pencil the over-all size, Fig. 6. Allow a trifle more than this so that the door can be trimmed. Mark the rails as in Fig. 7, placing the stiles in position and noting the shoulder length. Once again add a slight trimming allowance. This will give the front shoulder size, and the back shoulders must be increased by the rebate depth at both ends. Fix the parts together temporarily with a cramp as in Fig. 8 so that both are marked alike. Cut the joints before working the rebates, and make the fitting the final operation.

Level the joints when the glue has set and then fit. Plane the hingeing edge true, A, Fig. 9, and trim the bottom edge (B) so that it lines up with the carcase. Deal with the top edge next (C), and finally the lock edge (D). The edge of the latter should be at a slight angle so that it clears when it is opened (see Fig. 10). Allow slight clearance all round so that the door does not bind when polished. Do not remove all the waste from any one stile or rail, however. Otherwise the effect will be unbalanced.

This last detail is of special importance in the case of a cabinet with a pair of doors. All corresponding parts must finish to the same width as any discrepancy shows up badly.

STAGES IN MAKING DOOR WITH REBATED-IN PANEL.

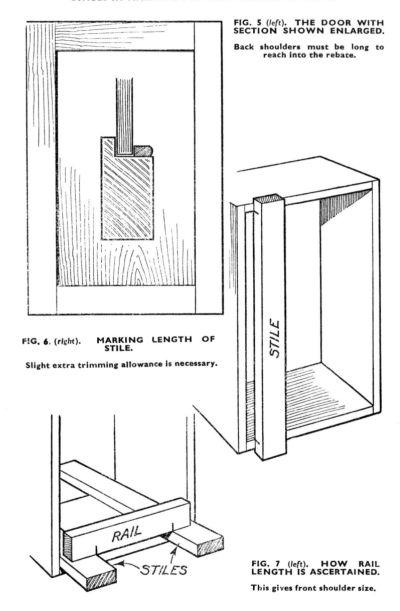

FIG. 5 (*left*). **THE DOOR WITH SECTION SHOWN ENLARGED.**

Back shoulders must be long to reach into the rebate.

FIG. 6. (*right*). **MARKING LENGTH OF STILE.**

Slight extra trimming allowance is necessary.

STILE

RAIL

STILES

FIG. 7 (*left*). **HOW RAIL LENGTH IS ASCERTAINED.**

This gives front shoulder size.

MARKING AND TRIMMING DOOR WITH REBATED-IN PANEL.

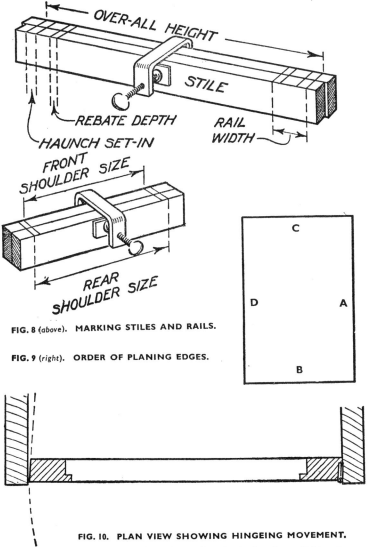

OVER-ALL HEIGHT

STILE

REBATE DEPTH

RAIL WIDTH

HAUNCH SET-IN

FRONT SHOULDER SIZE

REAR SHOULDER SIZE

C

D · A

B

FIG. 8 (above). MARKING STILES AND RAILS.

FIG. 9 (right). ORDER OF PLANING EDGES.

FIG. 10. PLAN VIEW SHOWING HINGEING MOVEMENT.

To enable it to clear, the opening edge is planed at a slight angle.

FLUSH DOORS

Solid butt-jointed door. If reliable, straight-grained wood is available the construction shown in Fig. 11 is sound. It is made up of a series of strips jointed together side by side with the heart sides arranged alternately front and back. This is levelled and veneered on both sides with a plain veneer, the grain running horizontally. Over this the final veneer is laid, once again on both sides. The

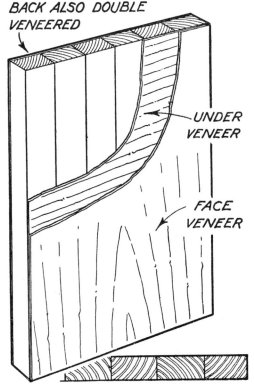

BACK ALSO DOUBLE VENEERED

UNDER VENEER

FACE VENEER

FIG. 11. FLUSH DOOR COUNTER-VENEERED ON BOTH SIDES.

The strips are arranged with the heart sides alternately front and back to minimise risk of warping. A door made in this way with sound stuff is reliable.

under-veneer is frequently omitted, but it makes a much more reliable job when it is included.

Clamped doors. These, Figs. 12 and 13, may or may not be veneered. They are satisfactory for quite narrow doors, but should be avoided for wide ones because of the liability to shrink and split. In any case sound, reliable wood is essential. If veneer is used both sides should be covered. In cheap work the tenons are omitted, the joint being the simple tongue and groove.

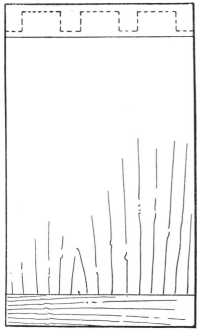

FIG. 12.   CLAMPED FLUSH DOOR.

If sound, seasoned wood is used, this is successful for narrow doors, but is risky for large ones owing to the shrinkage of the main panel being opposed by the clamps.

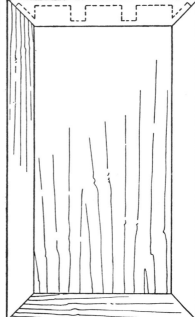

FIG. 13.   DOOR WITH MITRED CLAMPS.

Similar to above but with clamps mitred. The sides are generally made as separate pieces jointed on as otherwise it is difficult to cut the tenons.

FIG. 14. FLUSH PANEL FRAMED DOOR.

Suitable for narrow doors only. Sound, dry stuff is essential to avoid splitting due to shrinkage. Grandfather clock doors were frequently made in this way.

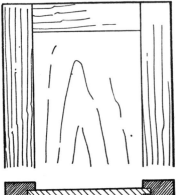

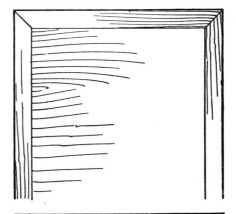

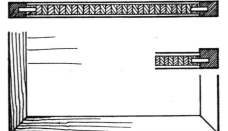

FIG. 15. LAMIN-BOARD DOOR.

The laminated board has a substantial lipping tongued round. This conceals the edges and provides a good fixing for the hinges. The lipping can be thicker than the panel.

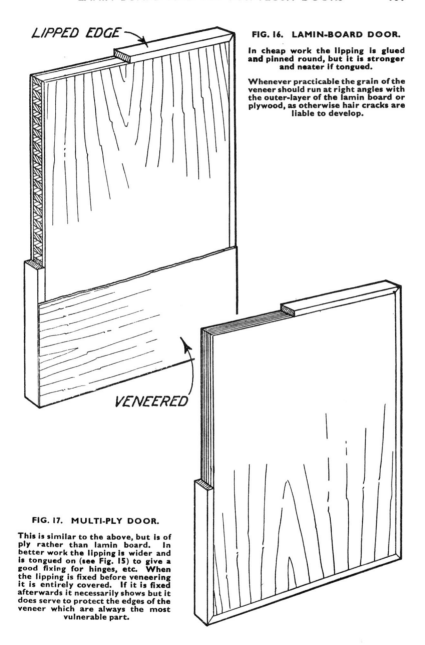

LIPPED EDGE

VENEERED

FIG. 16. LAMIN-BOARD DOOR.

In cheap work the lipping is glued and pinned round, but it is stronger and neater if tongued.

Whenever practicable the grain of the veneer should run at right angles with the outer-layer of the lamin board or plywood, as otherwise hair cracks are liable to develop.

FIG. 17. MULTI-PLY DOOR.

This is similar to the above, but is of ply rather than lamin board. In better work the lipping is wider and is tongued on (see Fig. 15) to give a good fixing for hinges, etc. When the lipping is fixed before veneering it is entirely covered. If it is fixed afterwards it necessarily shows but it does serve to protect the edges of the veneer which are always the most vulnerable part.

Framed door. This is a plain grooved frame with flush panel as in Fig. 14. It is satisfactory for narrow doors.

Laminated board door. Most flush doors to-day are made with lamin-board because of its simplicity and reliability. It is veneered and the grain of the board should be arranged so that the outer layers are at right angles with the veneer grain, as shown in Fig. 16. The edges should be lipped (see page 155), this being done before veneering when it is desired to conceal the lipping. If lipped afterwards the lipping serves to protect the veneer.

Multi-ply door. Fig. 17 shows this. The general notes on grain direction and lipping given on the lamin-board door apply here.

Framed lamin-board door. This (Fig. 15) is virtually a simple lamin-board door with extra wide and strong lipping. The latter is tongued on and can be either the same thickness as the panel or thicker as shown. The corners are mitred and tongued.

DRAWER MAKING

Except for the cheapest work the dovetailed drawer is the only form of construction worth considering. Its chief features are

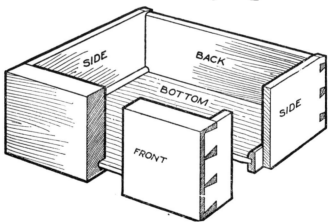

FIG. 18. MOST USUAL FORM OF DRAWER CONSTRUCTION.

Sides are lap-dovetailed to the front, and through-dovetailed to the back. Note how pins between front dovetails run almost to a point as in Fig. 19.

shown in Fig. 18, from which it will be seen that the sides are lap-dovetailed to the front, and through-dovetailed to the back. Note that the pins at the front taper almost to a point, this giving a very neat appearance. Even in machine-made cabinet work the drawers are invariably hand-dovetailed in good-quality work.

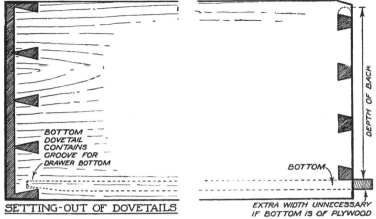

SETTING-OUT OF DOVETAILS

BOTTOM DOVETAIL CONTAINS GROOVE FOR DRAWER BOTTOM

DEPTH OF BACK

BOTTOM

EXTRA WIDTH UNNECESSARY IF BOTTOM IS OF PLYWOOD

FIG. 19. SIDE VIEW SHOWING HOW DOVETAILS ARE SET OUT.

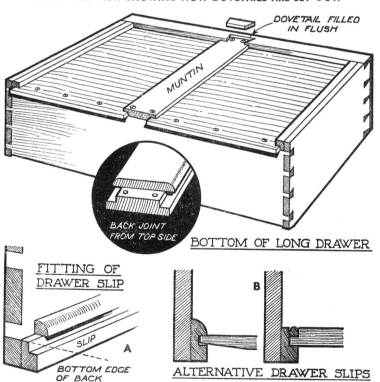

DOVETAIL FILLED IN FLUSH

MUNTIN

BACK JOINT FROM TOP SIDE

BOTTOM OF LONG DRAWER

FITTING OF DRAWER SLIP

SLIP   A

BOTTOM EDGE OF BACK

B

ALTERNATIVE DRAWER SLIPS

FIG. 20. HOW DRAWER BOTTOM IS FITTED, AND THE SLIPS USED

Several features should be noted in the setting out. Since the front is grooved at the inside to hold the bottom (Fig. 18), the bottom front dovetail must be low enough to contain it. Otherwise if it is opposite the pin it will show. The back rests above the bottom, and the lower square edge forms one side of the bottom pin. Grooved slips are glued to the sides to hold the bottom (A) Fig. 20. This saves weakening the sides by grooving them, and they increase the bearing surface, so reducing wear. For the general

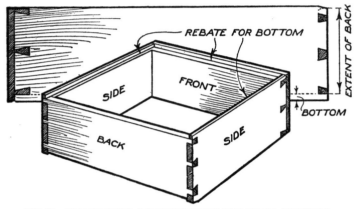

FIG. 21. ALTERNATIVE CONSTRUCTION FOR SMALL DRAWERS.

By fitting the bottom in rebates the utmost height is obtained.   Little trouble due to shrinkage will be encountered if the drawer is small.   If it is large, ply should be used for the bottom.

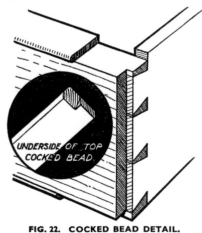

FIG. 22. COCKED BEAD DETAIL.

Ends and bottom fit in rebates.   Top is allowed full width.

run of drawers the fronts should be of $\frac{7}{8}$-in. stuff, the sides and back of $\frac{3}{8}$-in. wood, and the bottom $\frac{3}{16}$ to $\frac{1}{4}$ in., though these thicknesses would have to be increased for really large drawers. In the latter case— when a drawer is over 2 ft. or so in length a centre grooved rail or muntin should be fitted as in Fig. 20, dovetailed at the front and notched at the back. Nowadays plywood or hardboard is generally used for bottoms as it is free from shrinkage. If solid wood is used it should project at the back as in Fig. 19, so that in the event of shrinkage it can be unscrewed and pushed forward.

In small drawers where every fraction of space is needed the

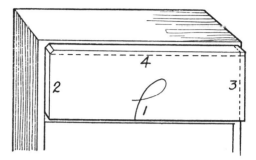

FIG. 23. FITTING FRONT OF DRAWER.
Figures show order of planing the edges.

bottom can be rebated in as in Fig. 21. Fig. 22 shows how the front is treated when cocked beads are required.

Making a drawer. The stuff can be about $\frac{1}{8}$ in. full in length and, say, $\frac{1}{16}$ in. full in width. Begin with the front, planing the bottom edge of this straight and square. Put a face mark on it, and plane one end so that it makes a true fit against the side. If

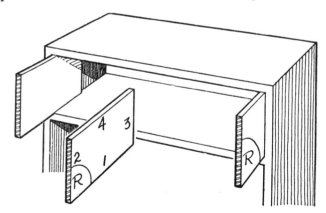

FIG. 24. ORDER IN WHICH DRAWER SIDES ARE PLANED.

anything the end can be planed a *trifle* out of square, small at the inside, so that it makes a slightly tapering fit. It should not be more than the thickness of a shaving. Holding the front in position, mark the other end, and plane this to fit as before.

The top corners can be chiselled off to enable the plane to be used on the end grain without splitting out. Finally, the width is marked and the surplus planed away. If carefully done the front can be pushed in until it projects about $\frac{1}{8}$ in. only as in Fig. 23.

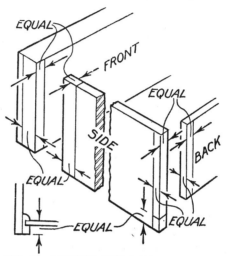

FIG. 25. GAUGING THE DOVETAIL JOINTS.
Cutting gauge is used throughout. In good work the gauge is used lightly only so that the marks are planed out later. The marks can be deepened locally if necessary to help the cutting.

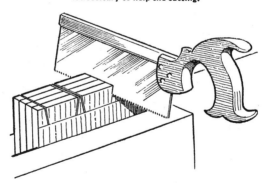

FIG. 26. SAWING SEVERAL SIDES AT SAME TIME.
Be careful to stop at the gauge line.

The procedure for the back is practically the same, but the width is reduced considerably. Remember that it stands *above* the bottom and is set down a trifle at the top. This is shown in Fig. 19.

The sides follow. About the same allowance in size is made. Plane the bottom edge true and make the front square with it. Each side should be marked R and L as shown in Fig. 24, so that it can be identified easily. Plane the back edges square, and place the two sides together to see that they are exactly alike in length. Finally gauge the width along the length. It can then be planed until it makes a hand-tight fit.

Dovetailing. Gauging for the dovetails follows (see Fig. 25). In order that the back may be positioned exactly the gauge should be set to the drawer bottom slip from the bottom to the top of the groove. The back edge of the sides is marked with it as shown.

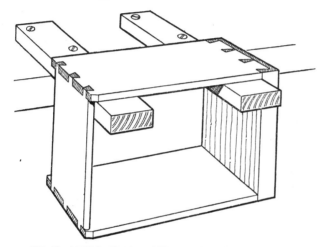

FIG. 27. SUPPORTING DRAWER FRAME WHEN PLANING.

Back dovetails can be chamfered. It eases running and allows plane to run right through without splitting out grain.

Mark out the dovetails. The two sides can both be sawn at the same time, or, if several drawers of the same size are being made, all can be cut together as in Fig. 26. The pins can be marked from the saw kerfs, putting the saw in each and drawing backwards. To avoid confusion it is a good plan to place the parts together loosely in the positions they are to occupy and mark the joining parts 1 : 1, 2 : 2, 3 : 3, 4 : 4, so that no mistake is made in marking out.

After chopping out the dovetails and pins, the groove in the front can be worked and the inside faces cleaned up ready for assembling, Do not hit the dovetails directly with the hammer when gluing as this will bruise the wood and probably cause splitting. Instead, place a block of waste wood over them and strike this.

C.M.F.B.—8

When cleaning up and fitting it is obviously important that the drawer is not racked about as this would break the joints. Fig. 27 shows how all risk of this can be avoided. Two pieces of stout wood are screwed to the bench to overhang at the edge. They are positioned so that the drawer just fits comfortably over them. In this way the side being planed is directly supported. To help in the running the back corners are usually planed off at a slight angle up to the dovetails. This will be found a special advantage when the sides are being cleaned up because the plane can be taken right through from front to back without danger of the grain splitting.

One point to remember when fitting a drawer is to make sure of exactly where it is tight before taking off a shaving. Excessive friction is usually revealed by the surface of the wood becoming shiny. It should slide just comfortably without undue slackness. No lubricant should be used when fitting. This should be applied only after the job has been polished. Candle-grease is excellent for the purpose. Oil should not be used ; it is liable to be dirty in use and may swell the grain.

DRAWER RUNNERS

When there is only one drawer in a carcase it generally runs directly on the bottom, and the top acts in place of kickers. In a similar way the cabinet sides are virtually the guides. When there are several drawers, or when the lower part is occupied by a cupboard, however, it becomes necessary to add separate runners, guides, and kickers.

The method of fixing these depends upon the cabinet itself. For instance, the fixing in a cabinet with solid ends is rather different from that in one having panelled ends, because in the former allowance has to be made for shrinkage.

Solid end cabinets. A reliable method for these is given in Fig. 28. The mid-drawer rail is grooved at the back to enable a dustboard to be fixed, but it incidentally provides a useful means of securing the runners, the front ends of which are stub-tenoned. When no dustboard is required the groove is cut in locally to provide a mortise in which the stub-tenon can fit. The runners are grooved with the plough at the same setting, then, when the stub-tenons are cut, it is merely necessary to make them line up with the groove.

The runners rest in grooves worked across the ends. This is essential for a really strong job because the grooves offer direct resistance to the downward pressure of the drawers. No glue is used for fixing, except the tenon at the front, because, in the event of shrinkage, the ends would be liable to split. The best plan is to glue the tenon and drive in a skew nail, partly to force the runner tightly home, and partly to hold it whilst the glue sets.   At the back a screw is used, the wood being cut away to remove the groove and to enable a shorter screw to be used.   Note that a slot is cut for the screw to enable the end to draw along the runner in the case of shrinkage, so avoiding splitting.   The screw serves to hold the runner in place rather than to provide direct support.

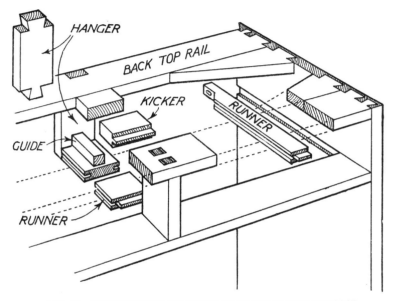

FIG. 28.   ARRANGEMENT OF RUNNERS IN SOLID END CARCASE.

Avoid glue when fixing side runners (except at front.)   Otherwise ends may split owing to resistance to shrinkage.   Screws at back fit in slots rather than round holes.   In first-quality work the lower drawer rail, runners, and a back rail with grooved-in dust board are sometimes made up as a complete frame.

The centre runner fixing depends in a measure upon the kind of back being fitted.   If there is a substantial muntin in the middle it is often possible to cut a groove across it and allow the back end of the runner to rest in this.   If this is not practicable the simplest alternative is to introduce a hanger at the back, as shown in Fig. 28. This can be conveniently dovetailed into the top rail.   At the bottom it is again dovetailed, this time into the runner itself.   The fixing at the front is by the stub-tenon as in the side runners.   Skew nails again are advisable to prevent any tendency to pull out.   Both edges are grooved for dustboards, and the back dovetail is set in at each side sufficiently to clear the grooves easily.

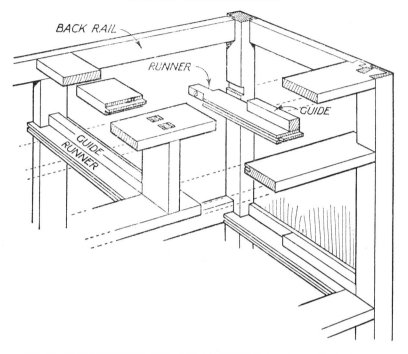

FIG. 29. HOW RUNNERS, ETC., CAN BE FITTED TO FRAMED-UP CARCASE.

Side runners are either glued and screwed to side rails as at bottom, or, if there is no convenient side rail, they bridge across between the posts, fitting in notches. Sometimes a supporting block can be glued to the panel, but the runner must not be glued unless the panel is of plywood and will thus not shrink.

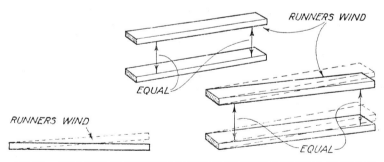

FIG. 29a. RUNNERS IN WINDING PREVENT DRAWER WORKING PROPERLY.

The guide is a plain square of wood glued and screwed directly on top. It is a good plan to make it slightly tapered in width to give easy clearance for the drawers. When there is a solid top to the carcase this prevents any tendency for the drawer to drop when opened. Sometimes, however, a couple of rails are substituted, as in Fig. 28, and this calls for the use of kickers.

One only is needed because the rails are built out in their width at the ends and provide the necessary support. The strongest method is to frame the kicker between the rails before the last named are glued to the ends. For cheaper work a stub-tenon can be cut at the front only, the back being butted. There is sufficient give in the wood to enable the tenon to be inserted and the back pressed down. A couple of nails can then be driven in askew, one at each side.

Framed-up cabinets. The method for a framed-up cabinet is rather different, partly because there is no shrinkage for which to allow, and partly because it is not practicable to have grooves because of the thin panels. A typical carcase is shown in Fig. 29.

The mid-drawer rails are tenoned into the posts and are cut round them at the back so that the ends touch the panels. This not only makes a neat, strong job, but it provides support for the runners. The back edge is grooved for the dustboard as in the previous example, and the runners are stubbed into this. At the back the runners are screwed to the posts, but it is advisable not to rely upon the screws solely—they inevitably allow of a slight movement. It is better to cut grooves, as in Fig. 29. This gives them a definite position and provides a strong bearing. The screw merely prevents the runner from pulling away. Note how the groove in the runner is cut away at the back to enable the screw to bed down.

Since the panels are necessarily set well in from the inner face of the legs, guides are needed on top of the runners. The simplest method of fixing is to glue and rub them in position, and drive in screws after the glue has set. They must not be glued to the panels.

The centre runner can be fixed to a hanger similarly to that shown in Fig. 28. In Fig. 29, however, a solid upright is shown, this forming part of the back framework. It is notched to hold the runner. When fixing the latter the stub-tenon at the front is inserted in the groove at an angle, and the whole thing pushed flat so that it enters the notch at the back. If the groove is shallow the wood will give enough to pass into the groove.

A bad fault to be avoided is that of winding runners as in Fig. 29a. It is not always easy to detect because top and bottom runners may be the same distance apart throughout. It is clear however that if both runners at one side run upwards the drawer will bind. To test for this, rest a strip of wood with straight parallel edges across the back ends of the runners and look across the drawer rail towards it. If in winding it will be at once obvious.

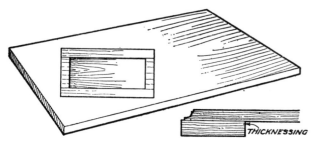

FIG. 30. SOLID TOP. THICKNESSING CAN BE GLUED TO UNDERSIDE.

It is essential that the grain of the thicknessing runs in the same direction as the main top to avoid shrinkage troubles.

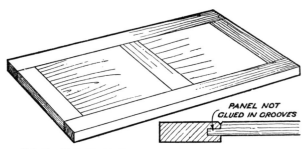

FIG. 31. FRAMED-UP TOP WITH GROOVED-IN PANELS.

This gives a flush top effect, except for the V grooves around the panel edges.

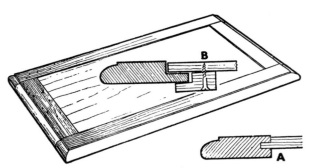

FIG. 32. CONSTRUCTION SUITABLE FOR WRITING TABLE.

Here the panel B can be fitted separately. The use of buttons for fixing allows for shrinkage and avoids splitting.

TOPS : TABLE, ETC.

There are one or two factors to be taken into account when making a top ; there is the kind of timber of which it is made, its condition, the purpose of the table or whatever it may be, whether the top can be fixed to a rigid framework or has no aid to keeping flat beyond its own construction, and whether economy is an important consideration.

Solid tops. Let us consider the timber first. If this is a sound, reliable wood and is well seasoned it can be used as it is, with little or no precautions. If necessary it can be thicknessed at the edges as in Fig. 30. Note how the grain runs in the same direction as the main top throughout.

If to be fixed to say a sideboard or similar piece the front only should be rigidly screwed, the back being screwed through slots to allow for shrinkage.

Framed tops. As wide timber is rare nowadays the framed top is generally used for tables as in Fig. 31. The main framework is in $\frac{7}{8}$-in. wood and the panels $\frac{5}{8}$-in. or $\frac{1}{2}$-in. grooved-in. They are not glued in because it is essential that they are free to shrink (they would be liable to split otherwise). The edges are either V-grooved or are beaded, so that a gap at the edge caused by shrinkage does not show. If ply or lamin board is used for the panels it does not matter about V-grooves. and they can be glued. It is assumed that the surface is to be veneered.

Another form of framed top is that in Fig. 32. It is used frequently for leather-covered writing tables. It is of course necessary to have a well-seasoned, reliable panel. If this is doubtful a good plan is to rebate the framework at the top and fit the panel as shown at B, Fig. 32. The leather cover is taken right over the edges and is fixed beneath. Then if shrinkage takes place the panel can always be removed, a slip glued along the back and the leather re-fixed. Note that buttons are used for fixing so that the panel is free to shrink. Plywood could be used, of course, in which case the grooved-in construction at A, Fig. 32, could be followed.

Clamping. A form of solid top which used to be very popular is the clamped type in Fig. 33. The main boards are tongued and grooved together to obtain the width, and at each end a cross-piece or clamp is fixed with tenons as shown inset. The clamp may be butted straight across, or it may be mitred as in Fig. 33. If sound, well-seasoned stuff is available the construction is strong and reliable. In the event of shrinkage, however, there will be trouble, the almost inevitable result being that the wood will split. The reason for this is that it is held rigidly by the clamps, yet is trying to reduce its width.

Lamin-board and plywood. The great advantage of these materials is their freedom from shrinkage. They can consequently be used as they are with just an edging applied. Lamin board is the better for the present purpose. Fig. 34 shows the construction. If the top is to be leather-covered for writing, either A or B should be followed, except that the panel would be recessed slightly to allow

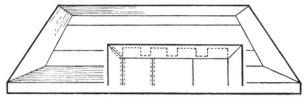

FIG. 33. SOLID CLAMPED TOP. JOINTS SHOWN DOTTED.

It is essential that dry, reliable stuff is used.

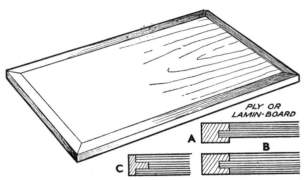

FIG. 34. LAMIN-BOARD OR PLYWOOD TOP WITH EDGING.

No shrinkage troubles have to be met here. The edging can be applied either before or after veneering according to the effect required.

for the leather. Both A and B are also suitable for veneering. C is another alternative, though the T-shaped edging is a trifle awkward to work by hand. This particular edging can be applied either before or after veneering. If before, the veneer passes over it and the whole thing is concealed entirely. If fixed afterwards it protects the edge of the veneer—a particular advantage in a table, the edge of which necessarily comes in for considerable wear.

CHAPTER V. VENEERING AND INLAYING

THERE are two main ways of laying veneer by hand as distinct from machine pressing : with the hammer and with the caul. Each has its own special uses and advantages, though they are largely interchangeable. Caul veneering is advisable for built-up patterns and veneers which are liable to cockle. The preliminary preparation of the groundwork is the same in both methods.

Cutting veneer. Most veneer nowadays is knife-cut and is comparatively thin. It can therefore be most conveniently cut with

FIG. I. CHIEF TOOLS AND APPARATUS USED IN HAMMER VENEERING.

The items shown include veneering hammer, knife, glue pot, toothing plane, swab, flat iron, and straight-edge.

chisel or knife. Lay it on a flat board and put a straight-edge along the place to be cut. Press well down and draw the knife across as in Fig. 2. When the cut is across the grain take special care at the end not to splinter out the grain. Press down tightly with the straight-edge. If trimming is necessary use a shooting-board, holding the straight-edge near the edge as in Fig. 3 to prevent buckling. The veneer should overhang the edge the merest trifle—not more than $\frac{1}{8}$ in.

Assuming that the veneer has to reach right to the edges of the groundwork, cut it about $\frac{1}{2}$ in. longer and wider than the finished size. Possibly jointing may be necessary to make up the width, and in this case the two pieces are cut to allow an overlap of about an inch.

Groundwork. It is imperative that this is properly prepared because any blemishes in it will inevitably show through the veneer eventually. Any knots must be cut out and the holes filled in with

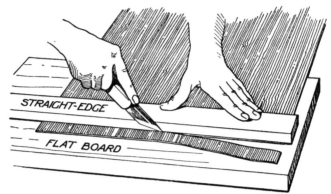

FIG. 2. HOW TO CUT VENEER WITH THE KNIFE AND STRAIGHT-EDGE.
The veneer must be placed on a flat board as otherwise it is liable to splinter
out over any irregularities.

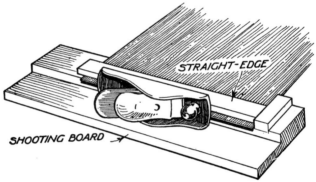

FIG. 3. METHOD OF TRIMMING EDGE OF VENEER WITH THE PLANE.
Give the veneer a slight overhang, and use the straight-edge to prevent buckling. The plane must be set fine.

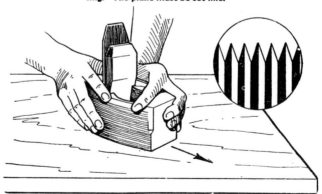

FIG. 4. PREPARING SURFACE WITH TOOTHING PLANE.
The plane is used diagonally first in one direction and then in the other.
This takes out irregularities and gives a key.

FIG. 5.   APPLYING GLUE TO THE GROUNDWORK WITH THE BRUSH.

Spread the glue as evenly as possible on both veneer and groundwork.
Avoid all grit and other foreign matter in the glue.

plugs, the grain of which runs the same way as that of the groundwork.   Any nail holes (there really ought not to be any) should be
filled with plaster of paris mixed with glue.   This is allowed to dry
out *thoroughly* and then levelled down.

Plane the surface perfectly true with trying or panel plane and
follow with the toothing plane.   The purpose of this is to take out
marks left by the plane, and to roughen the surface, so providing a
key for the glue.   Fig. 4 shows it in use.   The cutter is scored with
fine V-shaped grooves at the back so that the edge has a series of small

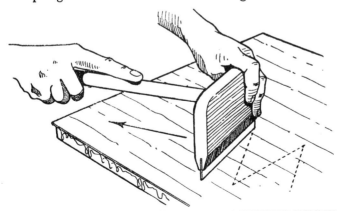

FIG. 6.   PRESSING DOWN THE VENEER WITH VENEERING HAMMER.

Work from the centre outwards with a zig-zag movement *with* the grain as
far as possible.   Glue is thus squeezed out at the edges.

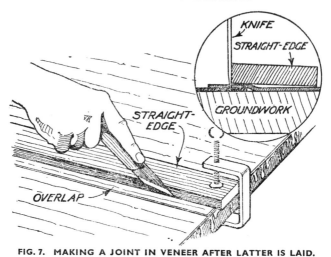

FIG. 7. MAKING A JOINT IN VENEER AFTER LATTER IS LAID.

The cut is made through both thicknesses where the veneer overlaps. The straight-edge should be held down with cramps.

points which scratch the work. Use the plane diagonally, first in one direction then in the other.

Good-quality plywood and laminated board both make excellent grounds. Remember, however, that the grain of the veneer should be at right angles with the outer layer of the ply as otherwise there may be a tendency for cracks to develop. Mahogany and similar hardwoods are successful ; oak is not quite so satisfactory as it is

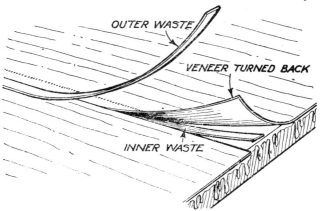

FIG. 8. REMOVING WASTE STRIPS OF VENEER AT THE JOINT.

Peel away outer waste, then turn veneer back to disclose inner waste, and peel this away. Press back veneers straightway.

rather coarse in the grain (it has been widely used, however, especially in period pieces) ; deal, if thoroughly sound, can be used, but should be sized after toothing to prevent the glue from being soaked up. Allow to dry before veneering. End grain should be avoided as a groundwork for veneer, but if it cannot be helped size it first.

HAMMER VENEERING

Applying the veneer. Apply the glue evenly to both the groundwork and the veneer as in Fig. 5. Do not use more than is necessary because all surplus has to be squeezed out. Place the veneer in position and press down with the hands, working from the centre outwards. This will get rid of most air bubbles. It helps to prevent casting if the back of the groundwork is dampened.

Dip a swab into warm water, wring well out, and lightly damp the surface of the veneer. In the meantime a flat-iron should have been warming up. Do not make it too hot ; only just enough heat is wanted to liquefy the glue and enable the surplus to be pressed out. The light damping with the swab prevents the iron from sticking, but use as little water as possible because this is the chief cause of casting. For a similar reason too hot an iron is to be avoided because it causes steam to be generated from the water, and this tends to cause the veneer to become pliable and stretch during the next process when the veneering hammer is used. This naturally means that it has to shrink correspondingly as it dries and so causes casting.

Veneering hammer. Immediately follow the flat-iron with the veneering hammer as in Fig. 6, working with a zig-zag movement from the centre outwards and in line with the grain as far as possible. If you work sideways you tend to stretch the veneer, and this causes casting, as the veneer subsequently contracts as it dries out. You will realise that you can deal with only a comparatively small area at a time because the heat from the iron is soon lost.

You can always tell when the veneer is properly down by tapping with the finger nails. A hollow feeling denotes veneer not in close contact. If after warming and pressing it still tends to rise you can cramp a flat block of wood over the place with a piece of paper beneath to prevent it from sticking.

Jointing. In hammer veneering the veneers are overlapped and jointed after laying. Lay the first piece as described, then the second so that it overlaps the first by about 1 in. Place a straight-edge along the middle of the overlap and fix down with a couple of thumb-screws. With knife or chisel cut through both thicknesses as shown in Fig. 7. The one waste strip can be peeled away immediately, and the other can be removed by raising the veneer as in Fig. 8.

Press down again with the hammer straightway, and stick gummed tape along the joint to prevent it from opening as the glue dries out.

Cleaning up. This is done with the scraper. Allow as long as possible for the glue to harden—twenty-fours hours is a minimum. Remove any tape or glue paper by damping lightly, allow to dry again, and use the scraper sharpened to a keen edge. Follow with glasspaper wrapped round the cork rubber, first *Fine* 2, then *No.* 1, unless the veneer is of a specially fine quality such as burr walnut, which has no special direction of grain. In this case use nothing coarser than *No.* 1, and finish off with *No.* 00, working the rubber with a circular movement. Some craftsmen clean up veneer first with a smoothing plane set fine, following with scraper and glasspaper. It gives a flatter finish.

CAUL VENEERING

This method should be followed for all tricky veneers which are liable to buckle badly if laid with the hammer, and for built-up

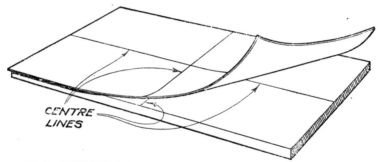

FIG. 9. HOW BUILT-UP PATTERNS AND MARQUETRY ARE CENTRED.
When the veneer must lie in an exact position centre lines are drawn on both it and the ground work and these made to coincide.

patterns, marquetry, and so on. In brief, what happens is that the veneer is glued and held temporarily with veneer pins. The caul, a flat piece of wood slightly larger than the work, is heated and cramped down with newspaper interposed so that all surplus glue is squeezed out and the veneer brought into close contact with the groundwork.

The preparation of the latter is the same as already described for hammer veneering. Both veneer and groundwork are glued and set aside to chill. The veneer is placed in position, and in the case of a built-up pattern or marquetry is held with one or two veneer pins. Fig. 9 shows how centre lines on both veneer and groundwork enable the exact position to be obtained.

It is important that the caul is flat and free from any indentations. Since it is imperative that the glue is pressed from the centre out-

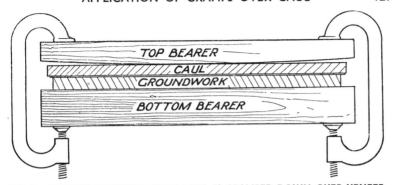

FIG. 10. SECTION SHOWING HOW CAUL IS CRAMPED DOWN OVER VENEER.

Note that the bottom edge of the bearer is curved so that pressure is applied at centre first
Bottom bearer is extra stout.

wards slightly curved bearers are used at the top as in Fig. 10. Thus when the cramps are tightened the pressure is felt at the centre first and works outwards. For the same reason the middle bearers are tightened before those at the ends (see Fig. 11). The bottom bearers are much heavier than those at the top so that only the top ones bend. The work thus remains flat.

Owing to the tendency for veneer to pull the groundwork hollow it is advisable to veneer both sides whenever practicable, using veneer of the same thickness. The pull of the one side thus cancels out that of the other. Both should be laid simultaneously with two cauls.

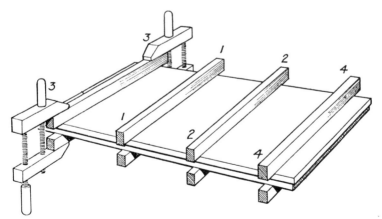

FIG. 11. ORDER OF TIGHTENING CRAMPS WHEN CAUL VENEERING.

By screwing down the centre cramps first the glue is forced from the centre out towards
the edges.

BUILT-UP PATTERNS IN VENEER

The method of making these varies to an extent with the particular pattern, and there is a certain amount of personal preference in the way the job is tackled. The examples given in Fig. 13 are typical and are fairly straightforward designs.

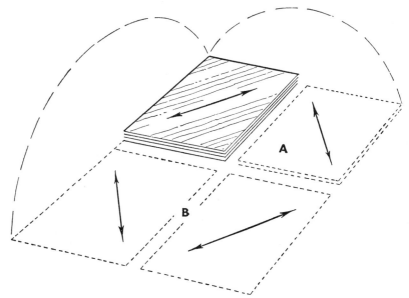

FIG. 12. HOW PACKS ARE " OPENED UP " FOR A QUARTERED PANEL.

Quartered Panel (A, Fig. 13). It is obvious that the direction of the grain must agree in all four quarters, and in the best work they are cut from four consecutive leaves of veneer, so that not only direction but variations in grain are balanced. Cut out the four pieces, keeping them with the same face uppermost and the same way round as cut from the flitch. Hold them together and plane two adjacent edges straight and square on the shooting board, placing a straight-edge over them and pressing down, as in Fig. 14, page 124. If a fairly generous allowance is made at the outer edges the pieces can be held together with veneer pins, these being put into the waste parts. Should this for any reason be impracticable the veneers can be held together with three or four little pieces of newspaper covered both sides with weak glue and slipped between the veneers. A flat

FIG. 13. VARIOUS BUILT-UP DESIGNS IN VENEER.

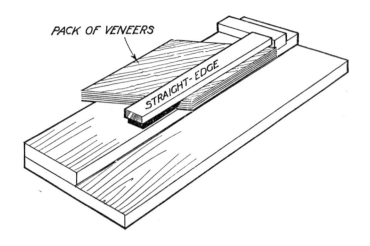

PACK OF VENEERS

STRAIGHT-EDGE

FIG. 14. HOW PACKS OF VENEER ARE TRIMMED.

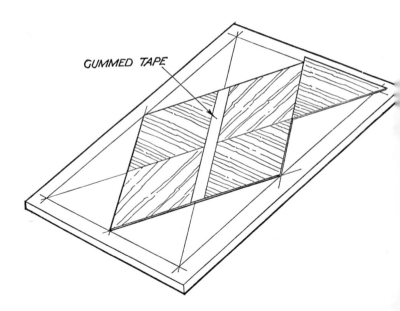

GUMMED TAPE

FIG. 15. ASSEMBLING DIAMOND PATTERN WITH GUMMED TAPE.

board with heavy weights above will hold the veneers flat until the glue has set.

They are afterwards separated as in Fig. 12, two being opened over sideways as at stage (A), and then the top two turned over lengthwise as at (B). The whole can be assembled on a flat board, and if the planing has been accurate the joints will be close. It may be necessary to take a shaving locally from the edges. If there is any serious inaccuracy it is necessary to correct all four quarters rather than plane the edges of just one, as otherwise the joints will not be in alignment. Gummed tape is stuck over the joints to prevent opening and the whole laid with a caul. It is necessary to position the veneer accurately as in Fig. 9, and two veneer pins should be tapped in to prevent movement.

Design (B) is somewhat similar but is rather more elaborate. The diamonds are prepared in packs, and it is essential to plane accurately to shape. The best way is to set out the pattern on a piece of paper fixed to the actual panel and take the shape from this. Fig. 14 shows one of the packs being planed, and the assembling on the design in Fig. 15. Hold the veneers down with a dab or two of weak glue, keeping closely to the design and making sure of close joints. If any correction is necessary make them as you proceed, but remember that any serious correction affects the other edges, and if it becomes obvious that the shape is badly out it is better to take a shaving from all the diamonds. Again hold the joints with gummed tape and lay with a caul. One important point is to keep all diamonds the same way round as when cut from the leaf. The reason is that some woods when polished vary in depth of colour according to the direction from which they are seen, hence the desirability of retaining the direction.

In design (C) the triangular pieces are again cut in packs as at (A), Fig. 16. They are then assembled as in the other examples with gummed tape. Allow the wide ends to extend about $\frac{1}{2}$ in. beyond the finished size so that the whole can be trimmed with straight-edge and knife, as shown by the dotted lines at (B). This necessitates cutting the projecting ends square at the sides, as otherwise they will overlap. Finally the end cross-grained pieces are jointed, fitted up, and taped.

The last design (D) is of a different character in that the main feature is shaped. The ellipse has to be cut out, and it is necessary to support the veneer between two pieces of material such as thin plywood. Thin plastic would probably do just as well. The whole idea is to support the veneer so that it does not crack. If two balanced panels are needed both pieces of veneer can be sandwiched. Set out the ellipse on paper by the pin and thread method and leave in the axes marks. These marks should be transferred to the veneers to enable them to be positioned accurately. The outline is sawn round with a fretsaw and the shape trued with file and glass-paper held on a flat block. When accurate the ellipse is fitted down on to the paper pattern and the " quarters " fitted up to it. The four can be fixed together as a packet with thin ply facing and backing, and the shape cut. The elliptical template already cut out can be used for marking. Fig. 17 shows the veneers being fitted.

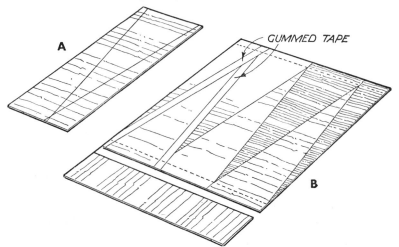

FIG. 16. TRIANGULAR VENEERS ASSEMBLED FOR DESIGN (C) FIG. 13.

It sometimes happens that an ebony or boxwood line has to be fitted around the ellipse. This is fitted after the latter is in position. A light smear of glue is put on at the edges, the line bent round and held with occasional veneer pins. The joint is spliced. Afterwards the quarters are fitted up. As the inlay is invariably thicker than the veneer, it is necessary to reduce it after it is in position before the whole veneer is laid. Otherwise the caul will press on to the inlay without touching the main veneer. A block plane set fine and used with care can be used. It is as well when laying the veneer with the caul to interpose several sheets of newspaper so that any inequality is taken up.

When a cross-banding is to be fitted around the edge, as in examples (B) and (D), it is often an advantage to add it after the main portion has been laid. It ensures that the cross-banding is of equal width all round, since the cutting gauge can be used to cut the veneer, this being used from the edge of the panel. This is especially an advantage when the banding is narrow, as any variation in width would show badly.

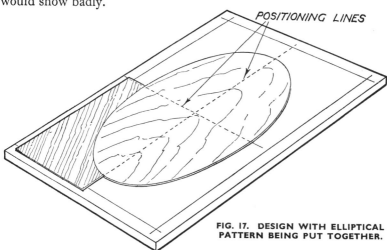

FIG. 17. DESIGN WITH ELLIPTICAL PATTERN BEING PUT TOGETHER.

COUNTER VENEERING

This consists of a double layer of veneer at each side. The inner veneers can be of a plain kind, and the grain is at right angles with that of the groundwork. Face veneers are at right angles with those beneath— that is, in the same direction as the groundwork. When the hammer is used, put the inner veneers down immediately one after the other, and allow to harden before face veneers are laid, again one immediately after the other. Tooth the surface of the lower veneers after the glue has set. Do not have the iron too hot or it may soften the glue of the lower veneer and cause it to rise.

In caul veneering both inner veneers should be put down simultaneously with two cauls. The face veneers are then

FIG. 18. STANDING GROUND-WORK AFTER GLUING BOTH SIDES.

added in the same way. It is possible to apply all four veneers in one operation, but it is safer to do it in two stages. In any case it is not practicable when there are joints in the lower veneers, because these have to be taped, and the tapes have obviously to be removed before the face veneers can be put down.

INLAYING

Nowadays this is generally confined to strings and bandings. These are obtained ready-made in a wide variety of sizes, woods, and designs, and the work consists mostly of cutting the groove or rebate to hold them and of gluing them. The scratch-stock is mostly used for working the groove (see below), the cutter being filed so that inlay makes a finger-tight fit in the groove it forms.

Having filed the cutter to size (its edges are square across so that it cuts in both directions) it is fixed in the scratch so that it works at the required distance from the edge of the work. Its projection

FIG. 19. USING SCRATCH-STOCK TO MAKE GROOVE FOR INLAY.
The cutter should be filed so that the inlay makes a finger-tight fit and stands only slightly proud.

should be such that when the inlay is pressed in it stands slightly proud of the general surface of the wood. Fig. 19 shows how it is worked with the notch of the scratch bearing tightly against the edge.

Working *with* the grain presents no difficulties, and if care is taken and the cutter kept sharp a groove can also be taken cleanly *across* the grain. For a large inlay, however, it is advisable to cut the sides across the grain with the cutting gauge. The chief points to watch are corners where the groove has to be stopped. The safest plan is to mark the extent of the groove with pencil, and work the scratch as close up to the corner as can be done with safety (see Fig. 20). A thin chisel can be used to cut right into the corner, the waste being removed with a small bradawl, after which the scratch can be carefully worked into the corner.

In the case of a fairly large inlay line to be fixed right at a corner, the rebate can generally be cut with the cutting gauge as in Fig. 21.

Set the cutter to slightly more than the inlay thickness and cut deeply in each direction. When the rebate is wide and shallow as for a banding, the width can be gauged and the bullnose plane used for the bulk of the waste. The scratch will finish it off and make it of equal depth throughout. Fig. 22 shows how the inlay fits.

Fitting the inlay. To take an example assume that a line is to be inlaid around a panel. With the mitre-square mark one end of the inlay and cut it off at 45 deg. Place it in position and mark the over-all length. Mark in the 45 deg. at this end and cut it with a

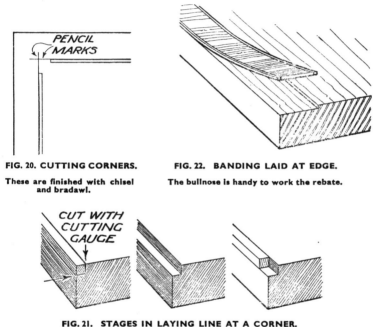

FIG. 20. CUTTING CORNERS.

These are finished with chisel
and bradawl.

FIG. 22. BANDING LAID AT EDGE.

The bullnose is handy to work the rebate.

FIG. 21. STAGES IN LAYING LINE AT A CORNER.

The waste is removed by cutting in each way with the cutting gauge.
It may need finishing off with scratch-stock or bullnose plane.

keen chisel slightly full. Try in position and cut off a little more if necessary. Go round all four sides in the same way. Fig. 23 shows the process.

Gluing. Place each inlay close to the groove in which it is to fit. Have the glue really hot and apply it to the inlay by drawing it with a single movement across the brush. Without loss of time place one end in position, press in with the cross-peen of the hammer, and rub straight down from end to end as in Fig. 24. Avoid loss of

FIG. 23. MITREING CORNERS OF BANDING WHEN INLAYING.

After marking the length, the line is drawn in with the mitre-square, and
cut with the chisel.

time because the glue chills rapidly. If the groove is the right width
there will be enough friction to overcome any tendency for the inlay
to spring upwards.

Generally the glue is tacky enough to hold even a wide banding,
but a thumbscrew applied locally will do the trick. In this case put
a piece of gummed tape over the inlay and adjoining surface to
prevent any tendency for the pressure to cause the inlay to drift

FIG. 24. PRESSING DOWN BANDING WITH PEEN OF HAMMER.

Work from centre outwards, or from one end to the other. Avoid
trapping glue in the middle.

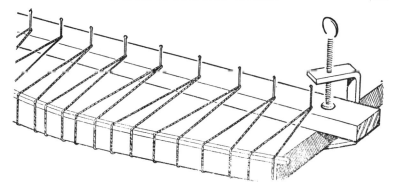

FIG. 25. HOW LINE AT CURVED EDGE CAN BE HELD IN PLACE.

The waste piece with nails is cramped on. After lacing with string the latter is damped, so tightening it.

outwards. This may easily happen when the inlay is being applied to a rebate rather than to a groove. When an inlay has to go around a curve it is bound to spring, and, to hold it in position, two wooden battens with a series of nails in each can be held at each side of the wood with thumb-screws and string threaded around them as in Fig. 25. After the whole has been tied on the string can be damped, so tightening it.

CHAPTER VI. DRAWING, CUTTING LISTS, MARKING OUT, ETC.

ABILITY to make accurate working drawings is of great value in cabinet work. It enables work to be marked with certainty, saves considerable time, and eliminates many possible errors. Scale drawing too is useful in that it enables proportions to be plotted in quickly.

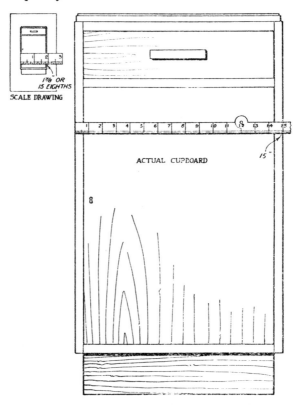

FIG. I. EXPLANATION OF WHAT A SCALE DRAWING IS.

The scale drawing is to a scale of 1¼ in. to the foot. Thus each 1¼ in
in the drawing represents 1 ft. in the actual cabinet.

Scale drawing. The chief value of scale drawing is that it enables you to reproduce in miniature the proportions of a full-size piece of furniture. It thus enables you to judge whether the

132

proportions are good, and to make adjustments quickly and easily. In important work a full-size design should follow so that the accuracy can be finally assessed before the job is put in hand, but the preliminary work can all be done in the scale elevation.

The most convenient scale is 1½ in. to 1 ft. because the drawing can be made with the ordinary 2-ft. folding rule. Since in 1½ in. there are twelve ⅛ths it follows that each ⅛ in. on the rule equals 1 in. on the full-size cabinet. Thus in Fig. 1 the actual piece is 1 ft. 3 in. (15 in.) wide. Consequently the scale drawing is 15-eighths (1⅞ in.) wide.

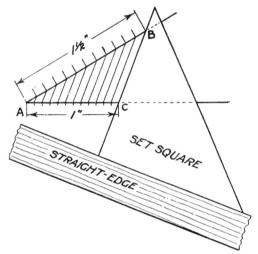

FIG. 2. SIMPLE WAY OF MAKING A SCALE.

This shows how 1 in. (AC) can be divided into twelve equal parts. Thus each division represents 1 in. in the actual cabinet.

Of course, other scales present no special difficulty, but you may have to make your own scale. For instance in a 1 in. to 1 ft. scale, since each inch represents 1 ft., you have to divide the inch into twelve parts, and the inches in the ordinary folding rule are not divided into twelfths. To make a scale of 1 in. to the foot draw a horizontal line and mark 1 in. along it as at AC, Fig. 2. From A draw a line sloping at any convenient angle—say 30 deg.—and, starting at A, measure 1½ in. to B and mark in the eighths. Place a set-square on a straight-edge and adjust the latter so that the square passes through the points BC. By moving the square along the straight-edge (which must be held still) draw in a series of parallel lines which will

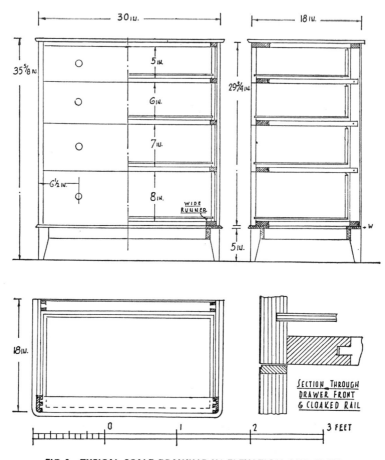

FIG. 3. TYPICAL SCALE DRAWING IN ELEVATION AND PLAN.

The front elevation is sometimes shown in part section. A plan is essential
in non-rectangular pieces.

connect the eighths with the 1 in. line AC.   Thus the 1 in. will be
divided into twelfths, each of which will represent 1 in. in the scale.

As a rule front and side elevations are all that are needed, though
sometimes a plan is a help, especially when the piece is not rectangular
in plan.   Fig. 3 shows a typical drawing.   The scale is an essential
feature, especially if someone else has to read the drawing.

Full-size drawing.   This may be undertaken to see exactly

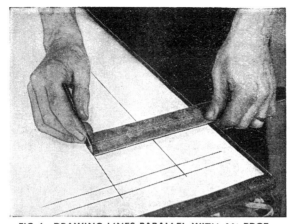

FIG. 4. DRAWING LINES PARALLEL WITH AN EDGE.

If the rule is kept square with the edge perfectly straight lines can be drawn.

what the piece of furniture will look like, to enable proportions to be adjusted, and to fix finally the various widths and thicknesses. Such a drawing is generally prepared on detail or cartridge paper, and when completed is stood up against the wall so that it can be properly seen. A large drawing-board is needed, and the long vertical lines are drawn with the rule and finger as in Fig. 4. The T-square is used for horizontal lines, and the set-square for short upright lines.

One important reason for full sizing is that it will enable you to make the piece without possibility of error, and to work out any problem of construction or detail or section. In this case you need show only certain parts in

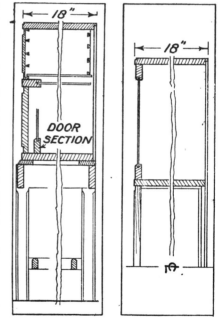

FIG. 5. TYPICAL ROD OR SKID.

Important parts are drawn in full size so that the various sections are clear.

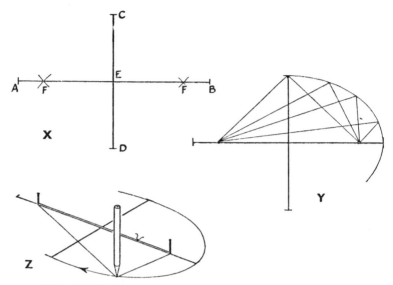

FIG. 6.   DRAWING AN ELLIPSE BY THE PIN AND STRING METHOD.

The axes AB, CD are drawn and the points FF put in.   Pins are inserted at F, F, and C, and fine string tied around them.   The pin at C is withdrawn and a pencil substituted as at Z.

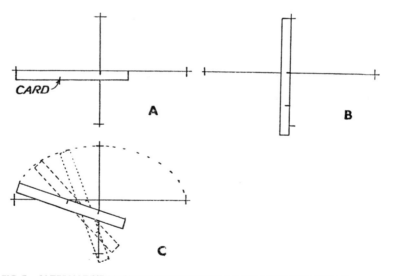

FIG. 7.   ALTERNATIVE METHOD OF DRAWING AN ELLIPSE WITH THE TRAMMEL.

After putting in the axes, half the length of each is marked on a strip of card with a straight-edge.   This is the trammel and is worked about the axes as at C.

full size.   What is known as a rod or skid is prepared.   All important sections are given in full size, but the full depth is unnecessary if the dimensions are put in.   Fig. 5 shows such a rod.   In some cases a second rod showing the plan is desirable.   If preferred, the job in its entirety can be drawn full size.   In this case plywood is preferable, especially for a big job, because otherwise shrinkage might cause an incorrect reading.

Setting out an ellipse.   For large ellipses the pin and string method is the best.   Draw in the axes AB and CD, Fig. 6, and, taking half the length of the long axis (AE) and measuring from D mark the points F.   Drive in panel-pins at the points F and C. Tie a piece of thin string around the pins as in Fig. 6, Z, and withdraw the pin at C, substituting a sharply-pointed pencil.   By moving the pencil sideways and keeping it within the string an ellipse is formed as at Y.

An alternative method suitable for smaller ellipses is that in Fig. 7. Draw in the two axes at right angles, and, holding a piece of card with a straight edge level with the long axis and level with the end, mark the centre on the card as at A.   Now hold the card along the short axis as at B and again mark the centre.   Then by keeping these

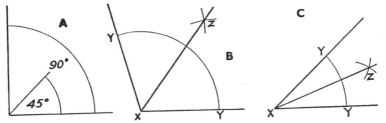

FIG. 8.   BISECTING ANGLES, A NECESSARY PROCEDURE IN MITREING.
The mitre square halves the right angle (A).   In odd angles (B and C) draw the arc YY from centre X.   With centres YY describe arcs to cut at Z.

two points always touching the two axes as at C a series of points can be made which form an ellipse when joined.

Bisecting angles.   As the essential feature about a mitre is that it must halve the over-all angle of the joining pieces, it is necessary to know how to divide an angle into two equal parts.   In the case of a right angle (A, Fig. 8) it is obvious that the mitre angle is 45 deg., and this can be set out with the mitre square.   Odd angles, however, such as those at B and C need specially plotting.   Set the point of the compass at X and describe the arc YY at any convenient radius. With each centre Y in turn describe two short arcs.   From where they intersect at Z draw a line to X.   This bisects the over-all angle.

Large circles. Large circles which cannot be drawn with compasses are best put in with a strip of wood with a nail driven through for the centre. A notch cut in the far end of the strip gives a definite position for the pencil as shown in Fig. 9.

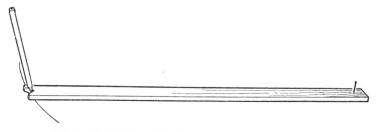

FIG. 9.   DRAWING LARGE CIRCLE WITH BATTEN AND PIN.

The pencil fits in the notch at one end.   Pin can be driven in at distance from it equal to the desired radius.

MARKING OUT, CUTTING LISTS, ETC.

Marking out. The preliminary marking out of timber is invariably done with pencil, and, in the case of straight lines, this can be conveniently done by planing the edge straight and using the pencil and rule method shown in Fig. 4. The finger acts as a sort of fence and keeps the pencil parallel with the edge. Cross-lines are put in with the square. Allowance must be made for subsequent cleaning up, and the general rule is $\frac{1}{4}$ in. in length and $\frac{1}{8}$ in. in width, though this has to be varied to suit circumstances. An exception occurs in rails to be tenoned at both ends. These can be cut to the finished length straightway because no trimming is needed, and to saw tenons longer than necessary and then cut them down afterwards is waste of time. In the case of rails having mortises at the ends, extra length is desirable because of the liability of the wood to split when the mortises are chopped. When a whole series of rails is to be marked allowance for the saw cut is essential in addition to that for trimming, and the best plan is to put in double lines as in Fig. 11 and saw between them.

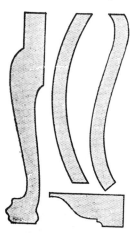

FIG. 10.   TEMPLATES.

These can be cut in plywood or card and kept for marking out.

In the case of shapes templates should be used. These (see Fig. 10) represent the over-all size, including any projections that may be needed for carving, etc., and the cleaning allowance. Considerable economy can often be effected by placing the templates as in Fig. 12 in which there is a minimum of waste.

Cutting lists. You can either buy your timber in boards and mark it out yourself, or you can send a cutting list to a firm which undertakes such work. The former is the cheaper method, but involves more work. If having the wood supplied to a cutting list, the latter will vary somewhat in accordance with whether the timber is to be supplied with a sawn or planed finish. Some suppliers follow the first system and others the second. Others plane both surfaces but leave sawn edges.

When the wood is entirely unplaned it is necessary to allow for finishing in the thickness as well as length and width. If you order 1 in. stuff you will find that it is under 1 in. already, and by the time you have planed it it will be no more than $\frac{7}{8}$ in.

If the wood is planed on both surfaces but is supplied with sawn edges you need make allowance in length and width only. This is by far the most usual system and is in many ways the most satisfactory. Much depends, however, upon the supplier. If the marking and cutting are careless you may find that the wood will

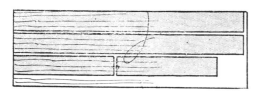

FIG. II. MARKING OUT STRAIGHT PARTS.

Remember the waste involved in the saw kerf, and mark in double lines as shown here.

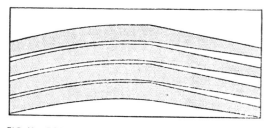
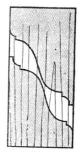

FIG. 12. PARTS MARKED OUT ECONOMICALLY BY JUDICIOUS SCHEMING.

By arranging parts to fit one inside or close against the other a considerable saving in timber can be effected.

not hold up to the width.   For instance if the wood for a long rail is slightly curved considerable waste will have to be planed off to make it straight, and it may finish too narrow.   The precaution then is to make extra width allowance if the suppliers are doubtful. Obviously, however, it is better to have a reliable supplier because otherwise it only means that you will be removing wood in shavings unnecessarily.   Naturally size enters into the matter to an extent since slight curvature on a small piece would scarcely affect it, whereas it would be serious in a long piece.

Timber which is supplied planed on both surfaces and edges should come to you finished exactly to the size you have specified and perfectly straight and square.   There is practically no trimming. Consequently very little allowance is needed.   Door stiles, for instance, can be ordered in their finished size.   Drawer sides might be $\frac{1}{16}$ in. over their finished width.

RULES FOR CUTTING LISTS

Give dimensions in this order—length, width, thickness.   This is recognised practice in the cabinet trade though the timber trade puts thickness first.

Add working allowance to lengths and widths, but give net thickness and say so.

Design your work to suit standard nominal sizes.

When parts have to be jointed give the over-all width (with trimming allowance added) and state on the list that one or two joints can be allowed, but that grain must be reasonable match.

In the final list for the timber supplier group all parts of the same thickness and in the same wood together.   Thus the supplier can see at a glance how much $\frac{7}{8}$-in. oak, etc., is required.

CHAPTER VII. TIMBER IN CABINET WORK

THE cabinet maker of to-day uses a much wider range of timbers than his predecessor of forty or fifty years ago. In addition to the traditional hardwoods such as oak, mahogany, and walnut, he has to be familiar with a whole range of comparatively newly imported timbers, some of which are listed on the following pages. In addition there are the softwoods frequently used for interior parts. The reader who wishes for fuller information should see the revised edition (1962) of the companion volume, *Timbers for Woodwork*.

Veneers. Much of the finest figured wood produced in exporting countries is converted into veneers. Indeed many of the richly coloured tropical timbers are available only in veneer form. Nearly all of it to-day is knife-cut as distinct from saw-cut, the reason being that there is little or no wastage, whereas in saw-cut veneer about 50 per cent of the wood is reduced to sawdust.

Manufactured timbers. Under this heading are the special forms of timber referred to later—plywood, multi-ply, lamin board, blockboard, hardboard, chipboard, and other materials which are now widely used for furniture parts. These do not call for tool manipulation in a way that is comparable to wrought wood, but their uses and advantages should be fully understood.

Characteristics. In any branch of woodwork one of the first things a beginner discovers is that, under the tool, every timber varies. This is found when the axe is laid to the base of a standing tree, when the two-handled cross-cut saw is used, when the log is placed on the circular saw bench, and later when the handsaw, the plane, and the chisel are used. Certain woods yield readily to the cutting tool ; others are obstinate and call for adjustment of the plane iron and frequent attention to the chisel edge. Some leave beautifully smooth surfaces ; others will remain woolly. Some split readily ; in others the grain is so dense that a screw breaks and the point is left buried in the wood. Some take kindly to glue or stain ; others resist. Some, under the polishing rubber, will leave a fine lustre ; others persistently refuse to smile.

It is useful to know the botanical *family* of timber. Later on, when one comes to learn of the different *species*, and then the numerous *varieties*, one understands what at first may often have been a puzzle. (The world produces over forty timbers classed as oak, some forty-five mahoganies, fifty eucalyptii, and nearly seventy pines.) It is well to know the source, whether home grown or imported, and is also a guide if the approximate weight per cubic foot can be ascertained. British oak, for example, is considerably heavier than American. Larch is nearly twice the weight of the Scots pine we commonly speak of as red deal, and a square foot of 1-in. rosewood might balance 2 sq. ft. of Honduras mahogany of the same thicknesses. The heaviest known tropical woods weigh nearly ten times as much as the lightest of all—balsa.

Supplies of imported timbers fluctuate considerably, largely for political reasons, so that it is impossible to say what may be available at any time. Some that were in everyday use before the war may be no longer available, and there may be others in use which were seldom used for furniture making. Taken as a general rule, the cabinet maker uses first-grade hardwood for show work, and second-class hardwood and softwood for interior or concealed parts. It depends largely, however, upon the quality of the work. In the best only first-grade hardwood is used throughout. The matter is affected too by the change in the technique of construction which has come about through the increasing use of manufactured materials—ply, lamin board, and so on.

In the following list no attempt can be made to exhaust the number of timbers that the home worker might possibly use for cabinet work purposes, but particulars are given of those more generally employed. For convenient reference the timbers are given in alphabetical order.

HARDWOODS

Agba (*Gossweilerodendron balsamiferum*). Sources: Nigeria and the Congo. Weight 30 lb. Colour, yellowish brown, sometimes reddish.
Qualities. Straight, even, and fine grain. Seasons well.
Uses. Cheaper furniture generally and interior parts. Stains well to resemble other woods.

Ash (*Fraxinus excelsior*). Sources: Europe generally, including British and Hungarian ash. Weight, from 46 to 47 lb. per cu. ft. Colour, yellowish white.
Qualities. Very tough and elastic with long and close grain.
Uses. Not widely used in furniture making, but is sometimes used for chair work. The American ash and Japanese ash are both lighter in weight than the European.

Beech (*Fagus sylvatica*). Sources: Europe ; also (*Fagus* *grandifolia*) East U.S.A. and Canada. Weight, 45 lb. Colour, light whitish brown or red.

Qualities. Close in texture and fairly hard, beech is noted for its silky and lustrous grain. It is durable under water, but, except when cut on the quarter, is liable to warp or twist. For steam bending it has been found useful, and it stands up well to boring.

Uses. In the furniture trade it has been used widely for chairs, for bentwood goods, and for turned easy chair and stool legs. Otherwise it is not widely used as a cabinet timber.

Birch (*Betula pendula ;* also *Betula pubescens*). Sources : Europe, Canada, Newfoundland, and East U.S.A. Weight, 43 lb. Colour, pale yellowish brown or red.

Qualities. Strong, tough, with a close and even grain, and fairly easy to work except in the case of figured wood. Takes glue well, but has a tendency to split readily.

Uses. A general utility wood, birch has been widely used for chair making, for tables, chests of drawers, cheap bedroom suites, etc. Birch plywood has been employed in enormous quantities for panelling of all kinds and other purposes. The timber takes kindly to stain, particularly to mahogany or walnut colour. For long the Canadian variety (called Quebec) has been regarded as the finest.

Black Bean (*Castanospermum australe*). Source : Australia. Weight, about 46 lb. Colour, olive-brown, often with very dark streaks.

Qualities. Straight grain, close texture, and rich figure. Works to a smooth surface and takes polish well.

Uses. This beautifully figured wood is known here chiefly in veneers, but locally is employed for furniture. The fittings and panelling of several important London buildings have been carried out in black bean. Supplies fluctuate.

Box (*Buxus sempervirens*). Sources : Europe, including British Isles, Asia Minor, Persia. Also (a different variety) Cape box, or East London boxwood, from South Africa ; Ceylon box-wood from India, Burma and Ceylon ; and different species from the West Indies, Mexico, and South America. Weight, from 54 lb. to 70 lb. Home-grown box is the heaviest. Colour, yellow, rather on the light side.

Qualities. Extremely close, even, and dense in grain with, when planed, a beautiful natural polished surface. The Abassian, Persian, and Turkish varieties are the best, the billets ranging to about 6 in. in diameter. Home-grown box rarely yields a diameter over 3 in.

Uses. In cabinet work these are now restricted almost wholly to inlaying and fine turnery.

Canary (*Liriodendron tulipifera*), commonly known in this country as American whitewood. Sources : U.S.A. (Eastern) and Canada. Weight, 28–29 lb. Colour, pale canary yellow. The timber is the produce of the " tulip " tree of America, but is not related to the tulip-wood of Burma or Brazil.

Qualities. Light in weight, mild, and easy to work. Is normally procurable in good widths and stains well.

Uses. Interior work generally, kitchen tables and cabinets, pianoforte work, inside cabinet work, etc. Sometimes used as a foundation wood for veneering.

Cedar (*Cedrela mexicana*). Sources : Central America and West Indies ; also varieties from tropical South America. An Indian timber, toon, is also a cedar. Weight varies according to kind from 27 lb. to 31 lb. Colour (generally), reddish, bearing a resemblance to mahogany.

Over the various cedars there is much confusion, some being hardwoods and others softwoods. The only one that concerns the cabinet maker is the Central American timber (as above), universally associated with cigar-box making. This, in colour and grain, has many of the characteristics of mahogany, but is lighter in weight and apt to be brittle. It has been widely used for drawer sides and backs and other furniture parts. As a foundation for veneers it is reliable.

The pencil cedars (*Juniperus*) from Africa and U.S.A. are junipers. The wood, pinkish red in colour, is the smoothest known ; this is due to a remarkably even grain. The so-called cedar of Lebanon is a conifer. So also is Port Orford cedar (known as " Lawson's cypress "). Western red cedar, although used for doors and all classes of joinery and outdoor work, is not a cabinet wood.

Cherry (*Prunus avium*). Source : Europe. Weight, 33 to over 45 lb. Colour, reddish pink. This is, of course, the wild cherry (or gean), not the fruit wood.

Qualities. Smooth, close grained, moderately hard, and works well under the tool. Imports, however, have always been small.

Chestnut, sweet (*Castanea sativa*). Source : Europe. Weight, 35 lb. Colour, light brown, closely resembling oak. Known also as Spanish chestnut, but in no way related to the familiar horse-chestnut which is not a cabinet timber.

Qualities. Taking an excellent polish, was at one time extensively used as a substitute for oak in the making of furniture. The grain is straight and close and is more easily worked than oak. There is no silver grain as in oak.

Ebony (*Diospyros ebenum*, etc.). Sources : India, Ceylon, Burma, Celebes, West and East Africa. Weight (according to variety), from 48 lb. to 77 lb. The African ebonies and blackwoods are the heaviest. Colour, brown to purple-brown and black. The ebonies are rarely handled by the home worker. Most are very dense, close, hard, and difficult to work. Only small pieces (the sap having been cut away) are imported, the supply of large logs now being exhausted.

Elm (*Ulmus procera*). Source : British Isles. Weight, 36–37 lb. Colour, light brown.

Qualities. Toughness, cross-grained growth, rendering it unsplittable, durability under water.

Uses. Although not a general cabinet timber, it has been used in recent years for mass-produced furniture. It calls for care and experience in seasoning if warping is to be avoided.

Wych elm (*Ulmus glabra*), sometimes called the Scots elm, is a superior wood, straighter in grain, milder, and less liable to shrink.

Fruit-woods. Incidentally, it might be remarked that the timber of our common fruit trees, apple, cherry, pear, and plum might often be used advantageously instead of sawing up the stems for fire logs. The older craftsmen understood their value for decorative work, and many fine examples of turned work from fruit-wood can be found not only in museums but in houses.

Gaboon (*Aucoumea klaineana*). Source : chiefly French Equatorial Africa. Sometimes incorrectly referred to as gaboon mahogany and known in France as okoumé. Weight, about 28 lb. Colour, rather a poor reddish brown.

Qualities. Light, but strong, and exceedingly useful for end and inside parts. It is widely used for lamin board and plywood. In the making of furniture in mahogany it may be freely used for all parts except the prominent show wood.

Gum or **satin walnut** (*Liquidambar styraciflua*). Source : U.S.A. Weight, 37–38 lb. Colour, pleasant light brown, often nicely marked. In this country it was common to designate the sapwood as hazel pine and the heartwood satin walnut.

Qualities. Even grain, light, and good working properties.

Uses. Cheaper and (preferably) lighter furniture, but seldom available to-day.

Holly (*Ilex aquifolium*, etc.). Sources : British Isles and Eastern U.S.A. Weight, 47 lb. Colour, ivory white. The grain is fine and close and the wood, which stains well, is excellent for inlaying.

Jarrah (*Eucalyptus marginata*). Source : Western Australia. Weight, 57 lb. Colour, deep red, tending to brick. Used in

Australia for cabinet work. The grain is dense and it takes a fine polish.

Laurel (*Terminalia tomentosa*). Sources: India and Burma. Weight 50–70 lb. Colour similar to Italian walnut.

Qualities. Hard and firm textured, durable and not liable to twist. Capable of a high polish.

Uses. Used to a limited extent for special furniture and chair making, but more generally for counters, panelling, fittings, etc.

Lime (*Tilia vulgaris*). Source: Europe. Weight, 37–38 lb. Colour, yellowish white. Need be mentioned only on account of its suitability for carving, the softness and even character of its grain rendering it almost unsurpassed for this purpose.

Mahogany (*Swietenia*, several varieties). Sources: (1) Central America ; (2) West Indies ; (3) South America ; (4) West Africa ; (5) Australia. Weights : (Honduras) 34–39 lb. ; (Cuban) 39–40 lb. ; (African) 30–48 lb. Colour, varying red.

Qualities. Mahogany still holds its position as the premier furniture timber, this on account of its strength, durability, compliant grain, rich colour, varied and beautiful figure, and its kindliness to stain and polish. The Cuban variety (*Swietenia mahogani*) has always been regarded as the finest but is difficult to obtain, and more widely used is the lighter-weight timber shipped from Honduras (*Swietenia macrophylla*). Other American mahoganies come from Costa Rica, Guatemala, Mexico, Panama, Tobasco, Brazil, Peru, Venezuela, Columbia, and other parts. The finest boards are converted into veneer form. Baywood, it may be mentioned, is a name given to certain mahogany shipped from Honduras Bay.

Uses. Furniture of every description.

The African mahoganies are derived from the tropical West African regions bordering on the Great Gulf of Guinea. Botanically they are of the *Khaya* species and, mostly, the commercial designations are taken from the ports of shipment. Thus we have mahoganies termed Axim, Benin, Cape Lopez, Gold Coast, Grand Bassam, Ivory Coast, Lagos, Sekondi, Sassandra, and many others. Their outstanding advantage lies in their length and width that are superior to those of any other kind. The grain has not the close firm texture of the American woods, nor has the figure an equal richness of variety. Furthermore it is not so reliable. It is readily and easily worked, however, and provides a valuable substitute for cheaper work.

Makore (*Mimusops heckelii*). Sources: Nigeria, Sierra Leone, Ghana. Weight, 45 lb. Colour, pinkish brown to purplish.

Qualities. Grain interlocked calling for care in seasoning. Reliable when dry. Usually available only in veneer form.

Uses. Good class work, panelling, etc.

Mansonia (*Mansonia altissima*). Source: Nigeria and Ghana. Weight 38 lb. Colour, similar to walnut, but fades on exposure.

Qualities. Strong and fairly close grained.

Uses. Moderate priced furniture. Its straight grain makes it suitable for legs, rails, etc.

Maple (*Acer*, various). Sources: Europe ; also U.S.A. and Canada. Weight, 37 lb. Colour, soft whitish yellow.

Qualities. Tough in texture and with a close non-fibrous grain. Takes a fine surface from the plane. The richly-mottled " bird's-eye " variety is rather harder to work.

Uses. Excellent for light furniture, small cabinets, caskets, boxes, and turnery.

Nyankom (*Tarrietia utilis*). Source: Ghana, Sierra Leone. Weight, 40 lb. Colour, somewhat like Honduras mahogany, but sometimes with purplish tone.

Qualities. Best quarter-cut boards are nicely figured, but quality varies, some being coarse grained.

Uses. General furniture and fittings.

Oak (*Quercus robur ;* also *petraea*). Source : Europe, including British Isles. The American and Japanese oaks also belong to the *Quercus* genus, but come under different species. Weights : (British) 45–52 lb. ; (Russian) 47 lb. ; (American) 41–50 lb. ; (Japanese) 40–47 lb. Colour, yellowish brown.

Qualities. These are so widely recognised that it is needless to elaborate them. Hard wearing and durable, its toughness is almost unsurpassed, and although inferior to ash in bearing strain it is one of the strongest and most serviceable woods for cabinet work and high-quality fitments. Its figure, too, when cut on the quarter has engaged the imagination from the earliest times, and it lends itself to almost every kind of finish.

Uses. Furniture, decorative woodwork, fitments, fittings, and joinery of every description. On account of an acid it secretes, highly corrosive to metal, care should be taken not to use it in direct contact with iron. Thus screws should be of brass, not iron.

Before the war the vast bulk of the oak used in this country was the American product, but imports have not since been resumed (1966). This is not generally of such a high character as the European oaks; but the timber is of sound quality and is admirable as a utility cabinet wood.

Obeche (*Triplochiton scleroxylon*).   Source : West Africa. Weight, 20-24 lb.   Colour, pale straw.   Very light in weight and straight-grained, this is used for drawer partitions, sides, and bottoms.   It stains well, but owing to open pores requires a stiff wood filler before polishing or varnishing.   It indents easily and is not suitable as a show wood.

Padauk (*Pterocarpus dalbergioides*).   Sources : Andaman Islands ; also, a slightly different variety, Burma.   Weight, 54–59 lb.   Colour, variable, but usually brilliant red, tending to turn brown or yellow on exposure.   A highly decorative wood, it has been utilised for panelling in this country, but not much for furniture.   Moderately hard, it is variable in its working qualities.

Queensland Walnut (*Endiandra palmerstonii*).   Source: North Queensland.   Weight, 46 lb.   Colour, usual walnut brown.

Qualities.   Medium textured wood, somewhat liable to twist in seasoning, but reliable when dry.   Tool edges are damaged quickly.

Uses.   General furniture, but is not popular in the trade as saw and cutting edges are quickly lost.

Ramin (*Gonystylus*).   Source: Sarawak.   Weight, 42 lb.   Colour, light yellow, tending to darken.

Qualities.   Generally straight-grained, and mild working.

Uses.   Cheaper types of furniture and interior parts.   Suitable for staining to match other timbers.

Rosewood (*Dalbergia*).   Sources : Brazil (known as Rio rose-wood) ;   also British Honduras, India, Java, and East Indies. Weight, 54 lb. and upwards.   Colour, rich purple-brown, at times very dark and banded with stripy markings.

Qualities.   Heavy and dense, with a somewhat open grain but an ebony-like surface.   One of its leading merits is the beautiful colour, but it is a difficult wood to polish on account of a tendency to develop minute cracks in the pores.   It is still in demand, however, by the pianoforte case trades, and on account of its superior decorative qualities might (when obtainable) be used for small show cabinets and boxes.   Much is imported for veneering.

Sapele (*Entandrophragma cylindricum*).   Source : East and West Africa.   Weight, 42–44 lb.   Hitherto—like gaboon—this was classed among the African mahoganies.   Resembling the premier wood in many ways, its colour inclines to a birch brown rather than to the usual reddish tint.   Most of it has a narrow stripy roe figuring which shows off as long parallel light and dark streaks.

Satin-wood (*Fagara flava*).   Source : West Indian Islands. An East Indian satin-wood from India and Ceylon is of a different species (*Chloroxylon swietenia*). Weight (West Indian), 51–52 lb. ; (East Indian) 53–62 lb. Colour, soft rich yellow.

Regrettably, comparatively little of this beautiful timber, so well appreciated by Sheraton, is now used in this country. Veneers continue to be imported, and the best is beautifully figured. The wood is dense, usually straight in grain, but is apt to take badly to glue.

Silky oak (*Cardwellia sublimis*). Source : Australia. Weight, 37 lb. Not one of the recognised oak family, this is an ornamental Australian timber of pinkish brown colour which has reached this country in fairly large quantities. Tough, elastic, and durable, it neither splits nor warps, and as it is invariably cut on the quarter the prominent medullary rays show a fine figure. It works easily, takes polish well, and for ornamental work may be recommended.

It may be added that shee-oak (or sheoak) and Tasmanian oak (known also as Victorian oak and stringy-bark) are well-known Australian timbers of different species, neither true oaks.

Sycamore (*Acer pseudoplatanus*). Source : British Isles. Weight, 38–39 lb. Colour, soft milk white.

Qualities. Invariably cut on the quarter to disclose a beautiful rippled mottle. The grain is close, even, and fine, and the boards have silky lustrous surface. In age the colour tones to light brown. Weathered sycamore is the normal wood treated with steam which darkens the colour to light brown.

Uses. The finest figured wood is now used chiefly for veneers, and thus sycamore is less in demand for regular cabinet work.

Note that the use of the word " plane " for sycamore is incorrect. The true plane is of a different family (*Platanus*) from which the heavily-mottled " lacewood " is derived. " Harewood " is a name given to sycamore (or maple) artificially dyed grey. This, however, should not be confused with the Indian " silver-grey wood," a name given to the darker heartwood of the Andaman, chuglam.

Teak (*Tectona grandis*). Sources : India, Burma, etc., and Java. Weight, 45 lb. Colour, brownish yellow when fresh, darkening with age. Streaks, almost black, are not infrequent.

Qualities. No other timber has so many ; this due to properties which enable it to withstand the vagaries of all climates. Neither for inside nor outside work does it call for protective polish, varnish, or paint, and it is resistant to warping or twisting. It does not develop shakes, and it defies attack from any insect pest. Hard, straight-grained, strong, and durable, it is fairly easy to work, although admittedly it will quickly dull the edge of plane iron or chisel. A resinous oil which it secretes (this with an unpleasant smell) protects it from rust when in contact with metal. On the other hand this oily nature prevents glue from adhering well. Surfaces to be glued should be wiped over with a degreasing agent such as carbon tetrachloride.

Uses. Being pre-eminently a constructional timber—all but imperishable—the first claim on teak is for ship-building, railway coaches and wagons, and general building purposes. Unfortunately its price in this country is exceedingly high, but it has been used widely for garden furniture—seats, chairs, tables, and arches. For indoor furniture such as smaller tables the cost would not be high.

Walnut, American black (*Juglans nigra*). Source: U.S.A. (Eastern). Weight, 37–38 lb. Colour, dark purple-brown, usually richly striped.

Qualities. Firstly, its excellent working qualities which make it pleasant to handle. Fairly hard, it is tough and inclined to be flexible. Not liable to twist or warp, it planes to a smooth surface and takes wax or polish well.

Uses. Every kind of high-class furniture, pianoforte cases, panelling, etc.

Walnut, European (*Juglans regia*). Source: Europe, including British Isles. Weight, 40–46 lb. Other walnuts are derived from Africa, Australia, Japan, and New Guinea.

Generally speaking, European walnut has a finer figure than the American, but on the latter we now rely chiefly for our supplies. British walnut is scarce, and the best European wood comes from Circassia (Caucasia), Italy, France, and Spain. The finest are obtainable only in veneers.

So-called "fancy" woods are invariably snapped up by the specialist. Among a few of these (mostly in veneer form) are: Amboyna, avodiré, cocobolo, king-wood, lauan, laurel, lignum vitae, marble-wood, meranti, olive, partridge, pear, purpleheart, sandal-wood, satinay, seraya, snake-wood, thuya, tulip, zebrano, zebra-wood.

SOFTWOODS

As, in the matter of names, a great deal of confusion has always prevailed, the following particulars may be helpful.

Pine, red Baltic or Scots (*Pinus sylvestris*). Sources: Northern Europe and British Isles. Weight, 26 lb. Colour, yellowish white.

As some seventy timbers go under the name of "pine" confusion is natural, and this (the premier softwood) is known here as red Baltic pine, redwood, red pine, red deal, yellow deal, Scots fir,

Scots pine—frequently just deal. In certain districts it may have other designations ; thus it is well to know the botanical name.

The timber is by far the most important in commerce. Our home supplies being very limited, we import it from the great forests of Scandinavia and North Russia. For building construction it is the standard wood : easily worked, strong for its weight, and durable. For general carpentry and joinery it is used universally. For cabinet work it is usually confined to back frames, interior parts, and so on.

Pine, yellow or white (*Pinus strobus*). Sources : Canada and U.S.A. (North-East). Weight, 26 lb. Colour, pale straw.

This is the once-famous yellow (or Quebec) pine, plentiful and cheap fifty years ago, but now scarce.

Spruce (*Picea abies*), alternatively called whitewood, white fir, or white deal. Sources : Europe, Canada, U.S.A. Weight, 28–34 lb. Colour, straw white.

Spruce, sitka (*Picea sitchensis*). Also called the silver spruce. Sources : Canada, U.S.A. This is one of the giant conifers which flourish on the Pacific side of North America. The average diameter of the stem is estimated at nearly 4 ft.

Douglas fir (*Pseudotsuga taxifolia*). Sources : British Columbia and U.S.A. (North-West). Weight, 32–34 lb. Colour, reddish straw. Again there is a complication of names, such as British Columbian pine, Oregon pine, Idaho pine, red pine, red fir, yellow fir, etc. Generally speaking, it has been found stronger than pine for constructional purposes, but is not quite so easily worked.

Larch (*Larix decidua*). Source : Europe, including British Isles. Weight, 47–48 lb. Colour, light to warm brick, often with interesting figure.

This is the heaviest of all softwoods and is used for such articles as bed-spring frames, meat safes, kitchen furniture, cupboards, garden seats, and other outdoor work.

Parana pine (*Araucaria augustifolia*). Source : South America. Weight, 30-34 lb. Colour, brown at heart, usually with distinctive reddish streaks. Available in clean boards free from knots, though poor quality is often knotty. Stands well when properly seasoned. Useful for general inside work.

Pitch pine (*Pinus palustris*). Source: U.S.A. Weight, 42–43 lb. Colour, reddish yellow. (Known as Southern pine in U.S.A.)

Qualities. Highly resinous, strong, and heavy. Clean and often handsomely marked. It is primarily a constructional wood, but has been used freely for church work, school furniture, and fittings in public buildings.

BUILT-UP BOARDS

These have largely superseded solid wood in many branches of cabinet work, especially veneered work. They have the advantage of being obtainable in large sizes, and of being free from the shrinkage troubles that belong to solid wood. It should be remembered, however, that the quality varies widely in accordance with the purpose for which the material is intended. A cheap quality plywood may be satisfactory for a tea chest, but is useless for cabinet work. It will have all the failings of cheap solid wood and a crop of others besides. We may conveniently divide the materials under two headings, plywood and lamin board.

Plywood. Most plies have an odd number of layers—3, 5, 7, etc., and the grain of the alternate layers (or veneers as they are called) is at right angles. Occasionally there are four layers, in which case the grain of the two centre layers runs in the same direction. Three layers is the commonest in the thinner plies, and they may be built up of three equal thicknesses, or the centre layer may be thicker

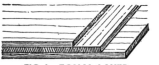

FIG. I.   EQUAL LAYER
PLYWOOD.

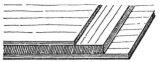

FIG. 2.   STOUT-HEART
PLYWOOD.

than the others to make up for there being only one. In this case it is generally termed " stout heart " (Fig. 2). Five-ply is sometimes made on similar lines (Fig. 4). When there are many layers it is generally termed multi-ply. For all practical purposes the latter is equally strong in both length and width.

The woods used in plywood manufacture vary widely, but the following are the commonest: birch, alder, ash, beech, gaboon, and various pines. Of these birch is the most widely used in cabinet work. Both this and gaboon mahogany are (in the best grades) excellent for best-class veneered work.

The care taken in manufacture affects the resulting plywood considerably. The cutting, drying, adhesive, and assembling all play their part. It is a thing about which you can do little, however, except to buy prime quality. This will be free of knots on one side at least, and it will have been assembled with a good-quality cement. It should also be free from internal defects such as those in Fig. 5. At A the bad core-joint results in the outer layers being pulled in, a defect which shows badly if it is veneered.   In B the core veneers overlap, resulting in a ridge across the panel.

Laminated board.   As shown in Fig. 6, the construction of this is rather different from that of plywood.   There are two outer

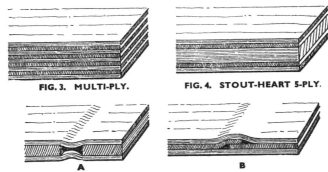

FIG. 3. MULTI-PLY.   **FIG. 4. STOUT-HEART 5-PLY.**

FIG. 5. FAULTY PLYWOOD TO BE AVOIDED IN CABINET WORK.

At A a depression is formed across the surface, and at B a ridge.

layers with a core sandwiched between them, the latter consisting of strips glued together side by side, the grain at right angles with that of the outer layers.   The strips are arranged with the heart on opposite sides alternately, so that in the event of shrinkage and consequent warping any pull in one direction is countered by the adjoining strips.

There are three kinds of boards, and we give them in the order of their quality.

Lamin board.   The strips forming the core should not exceed 7 mm.   It is the most satisfactory of the built-up boards, and is suitable for veneered work.   The full title is laminated board.

Blockboard.   This is a cheaper board than the above and is not so satisfactory for cabinet work.   The core strips are up to 1 in. wide.

Battenboard.   In this the core strips should not be wider than 3 ins.   It is unsuitable for good-class veneered work, though is often used for large cabinet backs, etc.

The drawback of both block and battenboard for veneering is that the line of the core strips is liable to show through to the surface of the veneer eventually as the wood dries out.   It appears on the surface as a series of waves.   The narrower the strips the smaller the waves, and it is for this reason that lamin board is superior to the others.   Even in this, however, the waves are liable to show to an extent, though an increase in the thickness of the outer layers in relation to the total thickness has brought some improvement.

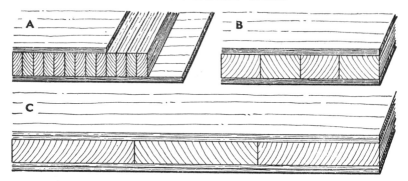

FIG. 6. THE THREE CHIEF KINDS OF LAMINATED BOARD.

A is lamin board proper, the core thicknesses no greater than 7 mm. In the blockboard B the core widths do not exceed 1 in. The cores in the batten board at C have a maximum width of 3 in.

Lippings. A drawback from which all built-up materials suffer is that the joints are bound to show at the edges. This necessitates their being edged or lipped, and a few ways in which this can be done are given in Figs. 7 and 8. The simplest lipping is that at A, Fig. 7, in which the strip is glued on, levelled, and the surfaces veneered. B has an advantage in that it is entirely invisible at one

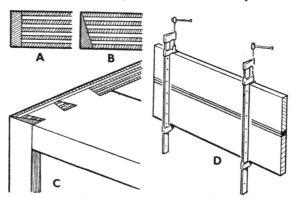

FIG. 7. SIMPLE EDGING FOR PLYWOOD OR LAMIN BOARD.

A is the simpler. B has the advantage of not showing at one corner (C). Simultaneous cramping is shown at D.

side, and is, therefore, handy for carcase work which is not veneered (see C). The lipping does not show at the outside. D shows how the material can be lipped in pairs.

A better form of lipping is that at A, Fig. 8, and its application

to thicker board is given at B.   For work to be moulded, C, D, or
F could be followed, the choice depending upon the required section.
At E is a method of thicknessing, and G is for a fielded panel.   Any
of the above could be cut by either hand or machine tools.   If, however, a spindle is available the section at H is specially satisfactory
since the canted edges protect the outer laminations.   Clearly it is
impossible for hand tools.

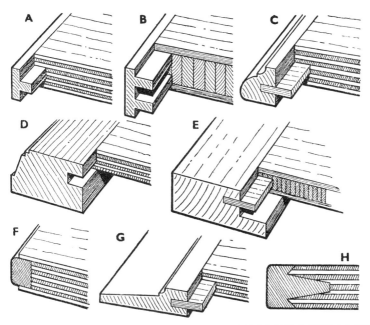

FIG. 8. VARIOUS FORMS OF LIPPINGS FOR PLYWOOD AND LAMIN BOARD

If lipped before veneering the veneer conceals the lipping.   If veneered first the lipping
protects the edge of the veneer.

A point to consider when lipping both plywood and lamin board is
whether to veneer before or afterwards.   The advantage of the
latter is that the lipping is entirely concealed.   On the other hand to
veneer first means that the lipping protects the edge of the veneer
(remember that the edges are always the most vulnerable part).
It is a point to consider in conjunction with the usage the work is
liable to receive.   A table top subject to much handling, for instance,
would be better if lipped after veneering.

For details of joints suitable for plywood and laminated board
see page 63.

C.M.F.B.—11

Chipboard. Improvements in the manufacture of this make it suitable for veneering, even for unsupported items such as doors, etc. Both sides should be veneered, and in the best work counter-veneering is desirable. In this the under-veneers have their grain at right angles with the face veneers as in Fig. 9. Lipping is generally necessary except for carcase parts, and most of the methods in Fig. 8 could be used, though it is advisable to avoid any method in which a tongue has to be worked on the chipboard because there is little strength in it. It is better to have the tongue in the lipping or to have a loose tongue. That at F would be unsuitable owing to the thin strips at the top and bottom being liable to crumble.

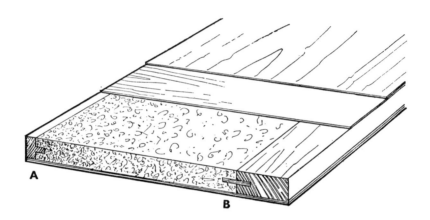

FIG. 9. CHIPBOARD PANEL COUNTER-VENEERED BOTH SIDES.

The lipping at **A** is little more than an edging to conceal the chipboard. That at **B** is more substantial and is used when structurally necessary.

The method of veneering is much the same as in solid wood, the surface being toothed first. Some makes of board, however, have larger chips at one side than the other, and it is advisable to have the small chips on the face side.

Chipboard does not take kindly to such operations as planing. It is therefore desirable to cut the board as close as possible to the finished size, leaving only a minimum to be trimmed. From this it is obvious that machine sawing is infinitely preferable to hand-sawing, which necessarily leaves a much more ragged edge.

Joints can be cut in chipboard, but generally it is better to regard it as panel material rather than for structural purposes. If the latter is necessary it is safer as a rule to joint solid wood edgings to it and cut joints in these. If dovetails are essential they should be coarse with pins about equal in size to the dovetails. Any attempt to cut fine dovetails will end in failure as the material would crumble. Similarly tenons are of little value in chipboard, as there is no grain direction as in solid wood, and the tenon would be liable to snap off. If a job needs a joint for which a tenon would be used in solid wood, it would be more satisfactory to substitute dowels.

Incidentally, veneering both sides of chipboard increases its strength considerably, especially when it is counter-veneered. It acts rather as a form of stressed skin construction. This, of course, does not increase the strength of joints, but it does stiffen the panel as a whole. Veneered panels should be brought to size before veneering, the reason being that if any attempt is made to plane or otherwise trim the edges afterwards the dust seems to be forced in at the sides, so that the veneer is liable to be pushed outward. This of course does not happen when a panel is edged, and is an additional reason for edging. The best procedure then for, say, a door is to cut the hardboard to size on the circular saw, less the width of the edging all round. It is then grooved to take the tongue of the edging, and the latter glued on. Both sides are levelled and veneered, and finally the door is fitted to its opening. It will be realised that the allowance for the edging should be such that shavings can be removed all round to make a close fit.

Hardboard. This is often used to-day in commercial cabinet work for drawer bottoms and panels of backs, etc., and for such purposes is quite suitable. When large sheets have to be fixed rigidly it is advisable to damp both sides lightly beforehand before fixing as otherwise it may swell and buckle. This seldom arises in cabinet work, however, since the panels generally fit in grooves and are relatively small.

CHAPTER VIII. GLUE, FITTINGS, ETC.

GLUE

NOWADAYS there are many varieties of glue suitable for furniture making, each having its own particular advantages. Let us consider them in detail.

Scotch glue. This is obtainable mostly in cakes, though some manufacturers supply it in powdered form. If properly prepared and used it is extremely strong, and it can be used for any wood without fear of staining. On the other hand, it offers no resistance to dampness. This, however, does not usually matter for furniture. It is an animal glue in that it is derived from the skins and bones of animals. The best form is made from animal hides, this sometimes being known as Salisbury glue.

The cakes should be broken up in a piece of sacking to prevent them from flying about, the pieces put into the glue-pot container and covered with water. It is allowed to stand overnight and heated the next day, when it will melt rapidly. Good glue will not liquefy in cold water, but it will absorb water and become jellified. A proper pot with water in the container beneath must be used. To place the pot over a naked flame is to ask for trouble. The glue is in danger of being burnt, and it deteriorates rapidly, especially if allowed to become too hot. A temperature of 150–180 deg. F. is about right for the general run of work. If a white scum appears on the surface during heating skim it off.

The consistency is important and is best tested when the glue is hot. If the brush is raised a few inches from the pot the glue should run down freely yet without breaking up into drops. It varies to an extent in accordance with the wood for which it is used. For a softwood it can be rather thicker owing to the pores of the wood being liable to soak up the moisture. Glue tends to deteriorate if kept at a high temperature for a long period, or if reheated many times. Consequently it is a mistake to prepare more than is actually needed for the work in hand

It will be realised that, although there is a limit to the temperature to which glue should be heated, it must not be allowed to chill, because this would prevent it from running into the pores of the wood. This means that to get best results the gluing-up must be done in a warm room free from draughts, and that the wood must be heated before the glue is applied.

Glue-pots and brushes must be kept clean.   Copper-interior kettles hold and retain the heat considerably better than those made from cast iron ; but in both types of kettle the interior should be tinned, otherwise the iron or the copper will turn the glue black or dark coloured.

It is possible to obtain a cold Scotch glue—that is, one which is used cold.   This is handy when a piece of work has to be glued up out in the open, or for a repair job which has to be done in a place where there is no means of heating.   For a white glue for light woods see note on page 161.

Casein glue.   This is supplied in powder form which dissolves in water, but, once allowed to set, becomes insoluble.   It is thus water resistant, though not waterproof.   An advantage is that it is used cold.   This makes the heating of joints unnecessary, and enables work to be assembled in a cold room or out in the open.   Furthermore, it gives more time in the actual assembling, because it cannot chill like hot glue.   This is a special advantage when a big job with many joints has to be put together.

On the other hand, the glue has a strong alkaline nature, and when used on woods containing acid causes discoloration and staining. Many softwoods and certain hardwoods present no difficulty, but oak, mahogany, walnut, and similar woods are affected badly.   The use of oxalic acid will largely remove the marks, but the result is liable to be patchy.   Some makers produce a non-stain casein glue, though not all of these are free from stain.   In any case they are usually not so water-resistant and are less strong than normal caseins. For such work as veneering ordinary casein glue should be avoided because it is liable to penetrate through to the surface and cause discoloration.   It can be helped to an extent by using the glue extra thick, and putting sheets of absorbent paper, between the veneer and the caul.   The cramps should be removed after about one hour.

In the preparation of casein glue the actual quantities depend upon the particular make of glue, and the instructions supplied should be followed.   The quantity of water is measured and placed in any convenient mixing vessel (not one of copper, brass, or aluminium). The glue powder is poured in and is stirred well for about a minute. It is then left for about half an hour (this again depends upon the make) and once again stirred.   It is now ready for use.

As a rule even rubbed joints should be cramped because rubbing is usually not sufficient to squeeze it out.   Apart from this it has not the tacky nature of Scotch glue.   In the case of veneering, a caul is essential.   The hammer cannot be used.   One point to remember in connection with casein is that only enough for the work in hand should be made up—or, at any rate, only enough for the day's work. In some cases it can be used on the second day, but it tends to thicken, and water cannot be added.

Synthetic resin glues. This form of glue combines the advantages of strength, high resistance to water and heat, and of being free from staining. Another advantage is that the rate of setting can be varied from a few minutes to many hours to suit the particular work for which it is required. The glue may be in powder form to be mixed with water ; it may be a thick, rather treacly liquid ; or there may be two distinct parts, the glue and the hardener. In the latter case the hardener may have to be added to the glue, though in some types the glue is applied to one part of the joint and the hardener to the other. For example, when a mortise-and-tenon joint is being put together, the hardener (a thin liquid-like water) is put on the tenon, the glue put in the mortise, and the two put together. No setting of the glue takes place until the hardener is brought into actual contact with the glue. In some makes of glue the hardener should dry on the wood first. In others it must be still wet when contact is made with the glue.

The time taken in setting depends upon the hardener used. Temperature also affects it, and advantage can often be taken of this since warming the glue accelerates setting. For small, simple work the quick-setting type is suitable since it enables the work to be cleaned up so soon after gluing. When assembling a large object such as, say, a sideboard, a slower setting hardener is desirable. One point to note is that the glue must not be kept in any vessel which has contained any substance of an alkaline nature as this affects the setting. Copper and brass containers are unsuitable. In regard to the hardener, metal containers should be avoided altogether. Glass, enamel, or earthenware are best.

Some synthetic resin glues can be used cold ; others must be hot-pressed. The last named are suitable only for such work as veneering in workshops where thermostatically controlled presses are installed. One type requiring hot-pressing is supplied in the form of a thin sheet like tissue paper. The advantage here is that, since no liquid is used in the process, all danger of casting is avoided.

Polyvinyl acetate glue (P.V.A.) is used widely today. It has the advantage of being used cold, and is a clean glue developing great strength.

Tube glue. Tube glue is not used much in cabinet work, but it is sometimes handy for small work. When pressure can be applied, or when there is no liability for the joint to spring, the work is best glued up straightway. In other circumstances it is better to glue both pieces, allow them to become tacky and then put together.

Bookbinders' paste. This is used chiefly when gluing down baize or leather coverings to table tops, etc. It can be obtained in both paste and powder form ; the former is preferable

Special cements. For cementing bone, ivory, tortoiseshell, and erinoid, the work should be wiped over with glacial acetic acid, after which it is glued and placed under pressure. Synthetic resin glue is ideal for tortoiseshell, but otherwise freshly made Scotch glue is quite good.

When it is desired to cement brass, iron, or glass to woodwork a fairly reliable cement can be made by adding a little plaster of paris to freshly made glue. A little garlic added to Scotch glue increases its strength for sticking metal inlays and helps to keep it fresh. Some workers recommend the addition of a little Venice turpentine to glue used for brass. There are also proprietary cements which are useful for metal-to-wood adhesion. Powdered chalk or flake white powder may be added so as to form a white glue when the joint on light-coloured woods needs concealment. For fixing rubber to wood use contact adhesive.

When glue is applied to the end grain of wood it is rapidly absorbed into the pores and it is advisable first to size-in the end grain by a liberal application of thin glue. This is very necessary where end-grain wood has to be veneered. In all cases surplus glue should be removed before it sets. The glue brush washed out in hot water is the best means of effecting this.

FITTINGS, ETC.—HINGES

Butt hinges. The butt hinge is by far the commonest in furniture. It is let flush into the wood and thus has a neat appearance. The flaps can be let in equally, or the entire hinge thickness can be cut in either the door or the carcase. It depends upon circumstances. At B, Fig. 1, for instance, the recessing could be conveniently divided, whereas at C this would not be desirable as the door stands in from the carcase face, and it would look bad to cut right across the projection. The entire thickness is therefore cut in the door, though it is usual to let the edge of the flap into the carcase to make it neater. This, however, does not affect pivoting. It is the knuckle position which counts.

Fitting hinges. To let in the hinge mark on the door edge the position, squaring the lines across in pencil. Assuming that the hingeing is to be as at C, Fig. 1, set a gauge to the complete hinge thickness at the knuckle Y, Fig. 1, D, and mark the front face of the door between the pencil lines. Reset to the width up to the

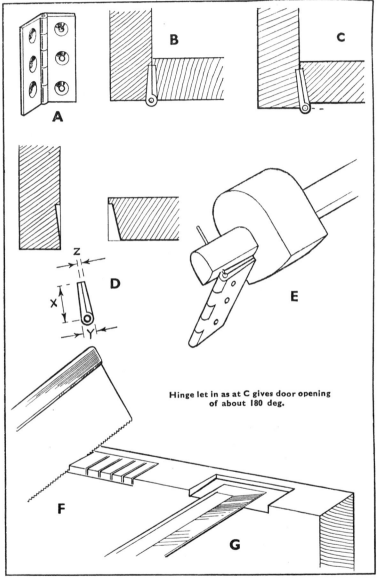

Hinge let in as at C gives door opening
of about 180 deg.

FIG. 1. STAGES IN LETTING BUTT HINGE INTO DOOR OF A CUPBOARD.

A. Butt hinge.   B. Hinge let equally into door and cupboard.   Note that door is flush at
front.   C. Hinge knuckle let entirely into door.   Latter is recessed slightly.   D. Sizes of
hinge to be noted.   E. Setting gauge to knuckle centre.   F. Sawing recess.   G. Paring away
the waste.

knuckle centre (X) less the amount by which the door is set in, and mark the edge. Saw the ends of the slot (F), and complete the cut with the chisel as at G, Fig. 1. Screw on the hinge using two screws only, and, placing the door in position, transfer the marks to the cupboard. Reset the gauge to allow for the recessing of the door, and mark. When the door is flush the same setting of gauge is used (distance X). Slope away the wood, being careful not to remove any wood level with the knuckle. Fix with a single screw at each hinge and try. Carry out any adjustment before inserting the remaining screws.

These butts can also be used for box lids, though special stop butts are frequently used, these opening through no more than a right

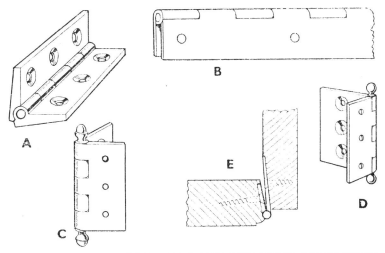

FIG. 2. VARIOUS HINGES USED FOR SPECIAL PURPOSES IN CABINET WORK.
A. Stop butt opening through 90 deg. only. B. Piano strip hinge. C. Acorn butt. D. Clock case hinge. E. How clock case hinge fits.

angle. Strip hinges of the piano type are used for some work. They are simple to fit since only a continuous rebate has to be worked. When it is necessary for the knuckle to project in its entirety, the acorn-ended butt gives a neat finish. A variation is the clock-case hinge which has one flap wider than the other to allow for the projecting door. These details are given in Fig. 2.

Special hinges. For bureau falls the back-flap hinge with its wide flaps is used. It is also used for the leaves of some extending tables, though a table with the rule joint needs the special hinge made for the purpose, this having one flap wider than the other so that it bridges across the hollow member of the moulding. The countersinking is also on the reverse side (see Fig. 3).

Reversible screen hinges have their obvious use. The only point to note is that the distance between the centres must be not less than the thickness of the wood. Otherwise the folds will bind. If it is a little more it will not matter so far as the movement is concerned, but it will leave a gap which is a fault in a draught screen. They are

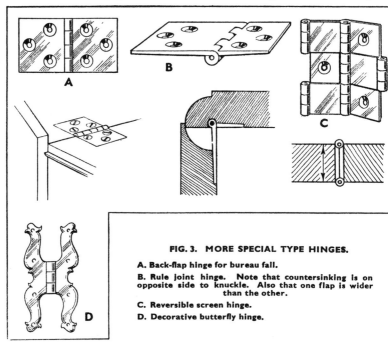

FIG. 3.   MORE SPECIAL TYPE HINGES.

A. Back-flap hinge for bureau fall.

B. Rule joint hinge.   Note that countersinking is on opposite side to knuckle.   Also that one flap is wider than the other.

C. Reversible screen hinge.

D. Decorative butterfly hinge.

let into the edges of the screen by a depth equal to exactly half the knuckle thickness. Butterfly hinges, being intended to be screwed directly on to the face without being let in, are generally of a decorative character.

Centre hinges. Sometimes, owing to some special feature of the work, it is impossible to use ordinary butts, and then the centre hinge is necessary. In Fig. 4, for instance, if ordinary butts were used for the left-hand door the thickness would swing over and prevent the other door from opening. The cranked or neck centre hinge brings the pivoting centre to the outer corner leaving the other door free to swing. Straight centre hinges are used when the centre is within the thickness of the wood. These are often used for heavy doors when there is a loose cornice. The centre is in line with the outer edge. It is imperative that the cornice is screwed on. Note that the hinges are made in pairs, that intended for the bottom having a collar so that the two plates have a slight clearance.

In addition, there are many hinges made for special purposes; cranked hinges for raised doors, card-table hinges, lift-off butts for dressing table mirrors, counter-flap hinges, and so on.

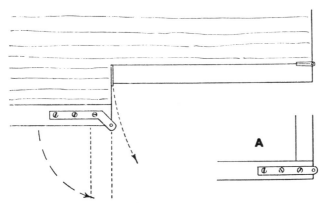

FIG. 4. PLAN OF CABINET FITTED WITH CENTRE HINGES.

In the cranked hinge the centre is at the outer corner of the door so that it does not foul the door to the right. The straight centre hinge is shown at A.

LOCKS

The commonest kind for cabinet work is the cut lock to be let in flush. It is in either horizontal pattern for drawers, or upright for doors. In the latter form it is made right or left hand. To tell which, imagine yourself facing the door at the outside. If the lock is to fit on the right-hand stile a right-hand lock is needed. The lock in Fig. 6, for instance, is right hand.

Fitting a lock. As the pin of the lock is not generally in the middle of the lock, it is necessary to position the keyhole in the centre of the drawer first, and mark the recess from this. Square a line across the top edge in the middle, and square it down the front for a short way. Set a gauge to the pin of the lock as at B, Fig. 6, and mark the centre line as at C. With a bit of the same size as the rounded top part of the escutcheon bore a hole right through the front where the lines intersect. Place the escutcheon on the hole, see that it is square, and tap with a hammer to make a light indentation. Cut down the lines with the keyhole saw, the latter on the waste side, and remove the waste with a small chisel. Tap home the escutcheon, making it a fairly tight fit.

Place the lock at the edge so that the pin coincides with the pencil line, and mark on the edge the position of the body of the lock as in Fig. 6, D. Gauge in the depth and width, and cut in the sides as far as the saw can be taken. Make two or three extra cuts between to cut up the grain. Chisel away the waste as at E, chopping down the sides where necessary. Place the lock in position and mark where the back plate comes. Chop down around the outline, and pare away the waste. The recess as at F is thus formed. Screw on the lock and cut the slot in the rail into which the bolt slides. To find the position of this, open the drawer and turn the bolt. Smear the end of the latter with dirty oil from the oilstone (or use something similar), close the bolt and shut the drawer. When the latter is home turn the key so that the bolt, in attempting to rise, makes a mark on the rail. The recess is best chopped with a drawer-lock chisel and large bradawl. In cheaper work a cupboard is frequently fitted with a " straight " lock, which is screwed straight on without being let in (Fig. 5). The keyhole should be cut first to suit the lock, and the latter then added.

FIG. 5. STRAIGHT CUPBOARD LOCK.

It is not recessed but screwed straight on.

Link-plate lock. When the door fits over the face of the cupboard it is necessary to use a link-plate lock (A, Fig. 7). Normally the position is obvious, the main plate of the lock being allowed to stand in a little way from the edge. Sometimes, however, the door framework is narrow as in a china cabinet, or the edge to which the link plate is fixed may be thin, and this may necessitate a certain compromise between the two. In extreme cases the inner edge of the lock plate may have to be reduced. The procedure for fitting is similar to that described for the drawer lock, but when setting the gauge to the centre of the pin allow it full $\frac{1}{16}$ in. or $\frac{1}{8}$ in. so that the edge of the main plate stands in. Bore and cut the keyhole and, holding the lock in place, mark the extent of the recess—as at C, Fig. 7. A gauge can be used to mark the sides. The recess can be partly bored then chopped with the chisel, the router being used to finish off. Note that spaces into which the bolt can shoot are necessary (D).

Screw on the lock, insert the plate and turn the key. If the door is then closed the position for the plate on the cupboard can be noted. As a rule it lines up with the main plate of the lock so that the position is obvious. It is advisable to check this, however.

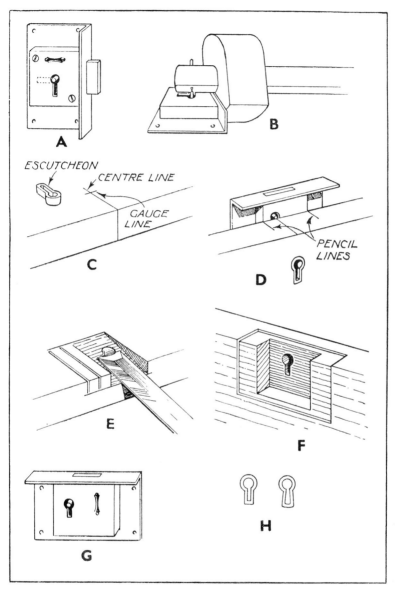

FIG. 6.   STAGES IN FITTING A LOCK TO A DRAWER.

A. Right-hand cut lock for door.   It has to be let in flush.   B. Gauging pin centre of drawer lock.   C. Marking keyhole position.   D. Marking recess for body of lock.   E. Chiselling recess.   F. Completed recess.   G. Cut drawer lock.   H. Modern and antique escutcheons.

Mortise lock. As the name suggests, the mortise lock fits in a mortise or recess in the edge of the wood. Its advantage is that it is not so easily forced as cut and straight locks. Either of the latter would give under pressure since the screws would simply be forced out. Square the keyhole position on edge and face, set a gauge to the pin centre, and mark as in Fig. 8, A. Bore the hole through to about the middle of the wood only, not right through. Cut in the

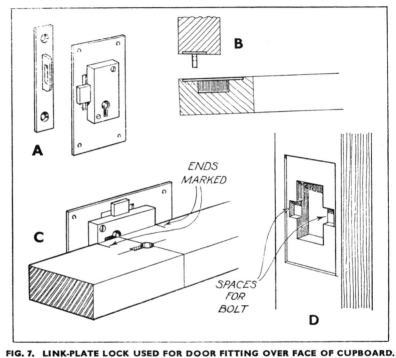

FIG. 7. LINK-PLATE LOCK USED FOR DOOR FITTING OVER FACE OF CUPBOARD.
A. Lock and its link-plate. B. Plan section showing how lock engages link plate. C. Marking position of recess for body of lock. D. The recess.

rest of the hole. Hold the lock level with the squared line and mark the ends of the body of the lock. A mortise gauge can conveniently be used to mark the sides. Much of the waste can be bored away, the rest being chopped. If the lock is then dropped in the plate can be marked round. The sides of the lock should bear against the wood and should not be a loose fit. Otherwise the entire strain is taken by the fixing screws.

Box locks. Box locks can be of either the cut or the mortise type,

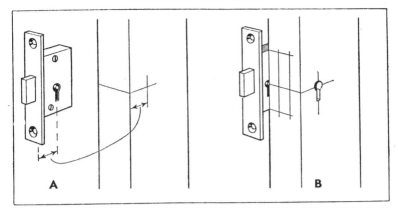

FIG. 8. MORTISE LOCK AND HOW IT IS RECESSED INTO EDGE OF DOOR.

A. Marking position of keyhole. Distance of pin from edge is gauged in. B. Mortise position is found by holding lock with pin level with keyhole.

and the marking and cutting is as already described. The only extra operation is that of fixing the plate to the lid. Put the plate so that it engages the lock, close the lid, and give the latter a thump locally. This will force the spikes on the plate into the wood so that the plate lifts with the lid. This fixes its position.

There are many other special types of locks, but the principle of fitting is founded on the main types given.

BOLTS AND CATCHES

There are two chief kinds of bolts ; the flush type and that to be screwed straight on. The former is the neater, but takes much

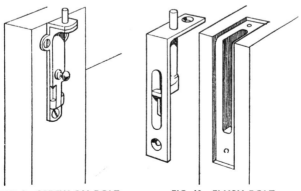

FIG. 9. SCREW-ON BOLT.   FIG. 10. FLUSH BOLT.

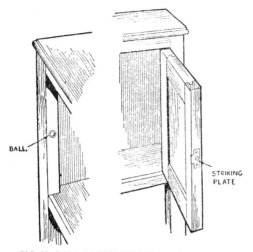

FIG. 11. BALL-CATCH FITTED TO CUPBOARD.

By putting the striking plate on the door instead of the cupboard it is concealed.

longer to fit as it involves rather awkward recessing. There is no special point about the cutting away. The simplest plan is to gauge in the sides and square the length, taking the sizes directly from the bolt plate. Cut in the latter, then chisel away the inner part so that the bolt clears the wood, working by trial and error. Some bolts are cranked for use in positions where the hole would be too near the edge. Both kinds are shown in Figs. 9 and 10.

Ball catches have become increasingly popular for doors, and the usual plan is to fix the ball to the door edge, and striking plate to the cupboard. The plate usually has a projecting tongue, the purpose of which is to take the wear of the ball, and it is generally an advantage to bend this over slightly. It may be necessary to file it back slightly. A rather more satisfactory arrangement is to fix the ball to the cupboard, and the striking plate of the door edge as in Fig. 11. The entire fitting is thus invisible from the front. The method is practicable only when the wood in the cupboard is thick enough to take the ball casing.

STAYS

There are many types of stays used for falls, tops, doors, etc., and their purpose is either to support the part or to limit its movement. The simple straight form is generally used when there is plenty of room inside for its movement, as shown at A, Fig. 12. In a more restricted space the rule-joint stay at B is the only alternative. A special form of combined hinge and stay is that at C. When there are separate lopers the stay at D can be used to give automatic opening. It is, of course, necessary to cut slots through the writing top at the sides. For supporting lids of cocktail and gramophone cabinets, etc., an automatic stay is generally used.

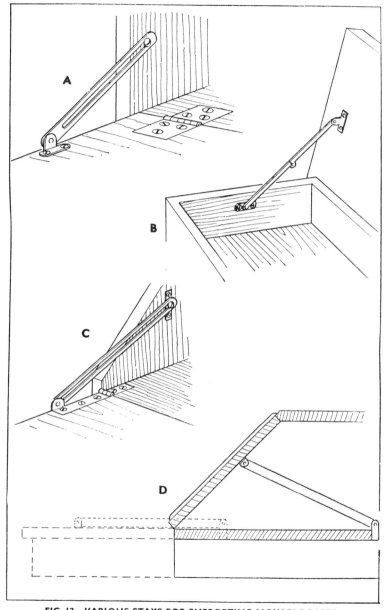

FIG. 12. VARIOUS STAYS FOR SUPPORTING MOVABLE PARTS.

A. Simple slotted stay for fall.   B. Folding rule-joint stay.   It is frequently more convenient to turn this with the knuckle projecting upwards.   C. Combined bureau hinge and stay. D. Stay for drawing out lopers.

TRACKS

Sliding doors are widely used in modern furniture, and a special fibre track is normally obtainable.   This is $\frac{1}{8}$ in. thick and is let into a groove worked in the cabinet.   Gliders let into and screwed to the door edge ensure a free movement (see Fig. 13, A).   For glass doors a

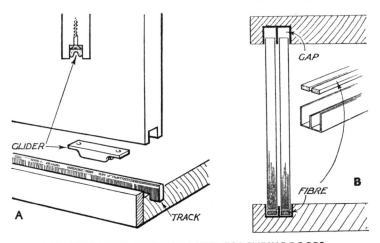

FIG. 13.   TWO TYPES OF FITTINGS USED FOR SLIDING DOORS.

A.   Runner fixed beneath door and sliding on fibre track fitting in groove.   B.   Metal E-section track with fibre bed for glass doors.

double metal track is often used (Fig. 13, B).   Strips of fibre in the lower track give a suitable surface for running.   The upper track is made extra deep so that the glass can be lifted up and dropped into the lower one.   It can thus be removed at any time.

CASTORS

These are made in many varieties, both in the form of fixing and style of wheel.   In the former connection there is the socket type, round and square, screw-fixing, plate-fixing, and steel-peg and collar form.   Wheels may be in metal, china, wood, or metal with rubber tyres.   There is no special point in the fixing of these except that socket castors must be an accurate fit since the strength comes from the fit of the metal against the wood, not from the fixing screws.

SCREWS AND NAILS

Screws. Apart from being available in various metals and finishes—iron, brass, copper, japanned, plated, and so on—screws are made in three chief forms ; flat-head, round-head, and raised-head. They are shown in Fig. 14, from which will be seen the way in which the size is determined. The gauge is known by numbers, and is the same regardless of the length. Thus a 1-in. No. 8 screw is of the same diameter as a 2-in. No. 8. When you order screws give all the details required, thus : " 2 doz. 1½-in. 9's, round-head, brass."

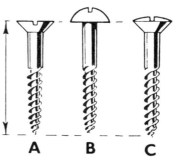

FIG. 14. CHIEF TYPES OF SCREWS.

A. Countersunk. B. round-head. C. raised-head. Arrow shows from where length is taken.

Generally iron screws are used. They are stronger than brass, but they should be lubricated, partly to make them easier to drive, but mainly to prevent rust. Vaseline or candle grease are both suitable. When brass screws are required it is better to drive in iron screws in the first place and then replace them with brass. Otherwise the resistance of driving into a new hole may cause the brass to break off. Countersunk or flat-head screws are mostly used in cabinet work, though there is a growing tendency to use the raised-head type in conjunction with screw cups for semi-show work, such as for fixing interior fitments, etc. Round-head screws are generally used in small sizes only for fixing certain fittings.

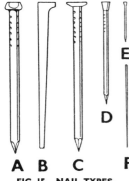

FIG. 15. NAIL TYPES.

These are the kinds mostly used in cabinet work. A. Oval wire nail. B. Cut brad. C. French nail. D. Panel pin. E. Veneer pin. F. Needle points.

Nails. The nails mostly used by the cabinet maker are :

Large work. Oval wire nails (A, Fig. 15) are used mostly owing to their having a small, neat head, and their freedom from liability to split the grain. Cut brads (B) and french nails (C) are used only occasionally.

Medium work. Panel pins (D) are the most widely used. They have a small head, easily punched out of sight. Small cut brads are handy when a nail with a stronger head grip is needed.

Fine work. Veneer pins (E) and occasionally needle points (F). The latter are of tempered steel, and after being driven in the required distance are usually snapped off.

Knock-down fittings. These are made chiefly to enable furniture to be made in sections for assembly at the retail shop or in the home. This is of particular advantage for export furniture, since space in transport is reduced to a minimum. Furthermore it simplifies polishing problems since awkward corners, etc., are reduced to a minimum. Another way in which " K.D." fittings are invaluable is in the manufacture of fitments, shop furniture, and so on. These are often large, and it is convenient to assemble the parts on the site.

There is a wide variety of fittings, and the work has to be designed to enable them to be used. There is no definite application, but generally their purpose is to enable carcase parts to be held together at right angles or in line with each other, or for fixing legs, etc.

Some of the fittings are shown in Fig. 16. That at (A) is for fixing parts together at right angles. It might be the sides of a cabinet to the back, or the sides to top and bottom. Round-head screws are used, these being driven in so that the plate can just move beneath the head. That for the parallel slot is in the middle of the slot; the other is centred in its slot at the round hole end. The plate is slipped into place, and is tapped down with a punch bearing on the projecting lug. It draws the parts together, and when right home the screws are finally tightened. There is a tendency to draw the part over out of right angles, and it is therefore assumed that both ends are being treated alike, and that there is a corresponding member at front or back (top or bottom) which holds the parts at right angles. It is an advantage when the one part can fit in a shallow rebate or groove, as this ensures exact position. A similar idea but for parts in a straight line is given at (B).

A device using an eccentric tongue is given at (C). The main body is let into the edge of the one piece, much as a mortise lock is let in, and a hole bored at the side to enable a screwdriver or key to be inserted. The other small shaped member is let into and screwed to the other part. Thus when the parts are put together the eccentric hook can be turned by inserting a screwdriver through the hole in the side. It thus engages with the shaped member.

At (D) is another fitting for the·same purpose, but here a bolt (tightened with a tommy bar) engages with a small plate let into the other part. Somewhat alike is the fitting (E), but here the bolt enters a threaded bush which is screwed into a hole in the wood. The metal plate is clipped over the head so concealing the fitting.

The device at (F) is for fixing table legs. The angle pieces engage in slots in the leg and are screwed. Screws are used to fix the parts with the lugs, the latter passing through slots in the angle pieces. Finally the wedges are tapped in, forcing the legs beneath the top.

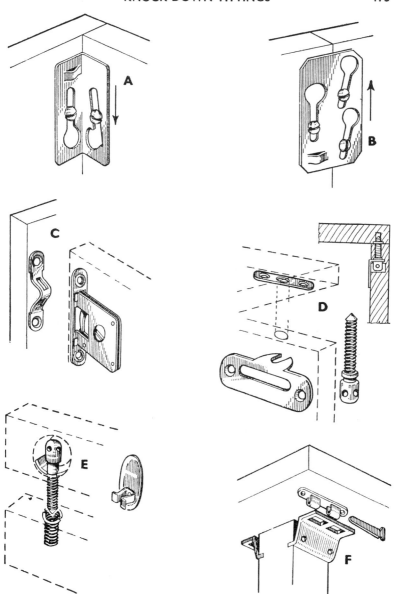

FIG. 16. SOME APPLICATIONS OF KNOCK-DOWN FITTINGS.

Although most of these were designed for specific purposes many of them can be used in other ways.

SHAPED MIRROR FRAME

THIS mirror relies largely for its effects upon the simple, graceful lines of the curves.   It will harmonise with almost any scheme of decoration, being at home equally in a modern interior as in one in period style.   It is made in solid oak with cross-veneer walnut facing.

FIG. I.   MIRROR WITH GRACEFUL, GENTLE CURVES.

Careful setting out is essential for a frame of this kind as it is to the gentle graceful curves that it owes its effect.   Anything in the way of overdone curves will ruin the appearance.   Fig. 2 gives the shape set out in 1 in. squares.   This can be taken as a general guide, but the shape must be faired in if an attractive outline is to be produced.   If a bent strip of wood is used to draw the curves, the thickness should be reduced at the ends, as otherwise most of the curvature will take place in the middle, and this forms an ugly shape.   This

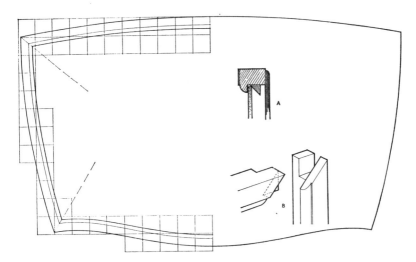

FIG. 2. SHAPE SET OUT IN I IN. SQUARES. A. SECTION. B. CORNER JOINT

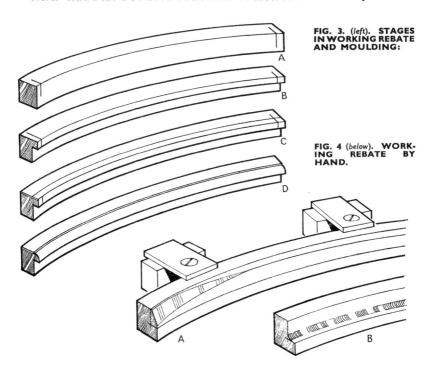

FIG. 3. (*left*). STAGES IN WORKING REBATE AND MOULDING:

FIG. 4 (*below*). WORKING REBATE BY HAND.

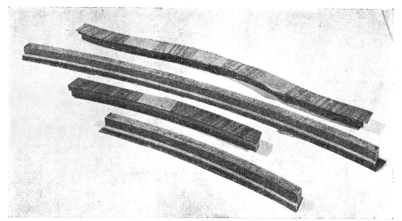

FIG. 5. REBATED PARTS AFTER VENEERING READY FOR MOULDING.

bent strip can be used also for the centre part of the bottom serpentine curve, but the ends need to be put in freehand.

Transferring the shape. Templets should be cut in card to enable the wood to be marked out, and these should be made about 1 in. longer than the finished size. A mark of the finished length should be made on them, however, and this also transferred to the wood. To cut the wood the machine bandsaw is the best method, but for handwork the bow saw is perfectly satisfactory. Cut slightly full to allow for any unevenness. Afterwards clean up the inner edge, making the edge square and the curve clean. This is shown at (A), Fig. 3 where it will be seen that the length sizes are marked. A gauge with round face to the fence is used to mark the width, and the wood trimmed down to this.

Rebating. The working of the rebate depends upon the facilities available. A spindle moulder or router is the simplest means, but if it has to be done by hand the wood should be held down as in Fig. 4 and a chamfer worked along the edge down to just short of the gauge lines as at (A). This is followed by a gouge cut as at (B). Finally a chisel is run along the corner to clean out the curve. Those who have a rebate plane with curved sole can use this to finish off, otherwise the final levelling can be done with coarse glasspaper held around a shaped block. Fig. 3 shows at (B) the wood with the rebate worked.

Veneering the surface follows. Pieces of veneer are fitted together and rubbed down with the cross peen of the hammer, care being taken to make close joints. Pieces of gummed tape are stuck over the last named to prevent them from opening as the glue dries out. A slight overhang on the veneer is allowed at both sides as in Fig. 5. When the glue has set the overhang at both edges is trimmed flush as at (C), Fig. 3. This also shows how the moulding depth is marked in with the cutting gauge, the width equalling that of the rebate.

Moulding. This follows, and here again either the spindle moulder or the router is the simplest way. For hand work the scratch-stock must be used. Whichever method is adopted a slight flat must be left as in Fig. 6 as otherwise the cutter is liable to chew beyond the line as there is nothing to stop it, whereas the flat does provide a bearing for the shoulder of the scratch-stock or the spindle of the spindle moulder. Tearing out of the veneer is prevented by the gauge cut on the surface.

Having cleaned up the moulding with glasspaper held around a shaped rubber (this incidentally takes out the narrow flat), the corner joints are cut as at (B), Fig. 2. It is a form of open tenon joint with mitre at the front. If this is gauged from the front the parts should go together level, leaving little cleaning up to be done on the veneered face.

Finish the whole thing with clear polish, either French or polyurethane. To hold the mirror triangular blocks are glued round as in the section in Fig. 2. In this way the silver of the mirror is not touched. Remember, as in all mirrors, to black the rebate first, as otherwise there will be an unwanted reflection. For the back either plywood or hardboard can be used.

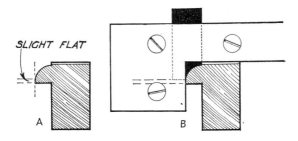

FIG. 6. DETAIL OF MOULDING AND SCRATCH STOCK.

BOOKCASE IN OAK

Through dovetails are used at the corners of the main carcase, and if carefully cut form an attractive decorative feature. Since the doors fit in a sloping rebate, however, it is necessary to have a mitre at the front deep enough to allow for this as at (B), Fig. 3.   Much the

FIG. I.   SIMPLE DESIGN WITH CLEAN LINES.

same applies to the back edges where the rebate to hold the back has to be worked.

Main carcase.   Prepare the two ends, top, and bottom to the over-all size.   It will probably be necessary to joint to obtain the width.   Although plain glued joints can be used, it is more satisfactory either to tongue or dowel the parts.   Trim all to size and mark out the dovetails.   In the early stage the gauge marks should be

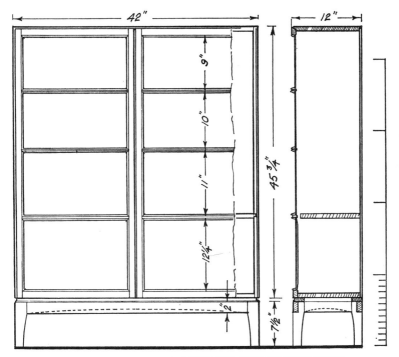

FIG. 2. FRONT ELEVATION AND SIDE SECTION WITH SCALE.

put in extremely lightly. They can be deepened locally later, after the dovetails have been sawn in. Unless this is done an unsightly cut shows across all the joints. The end cuts against the mitre are square.

Before the mitres are cut it is necessary to work the front and back rebates as otherwise the mitres may be damaged. To work the front sloping rebate a square rebate is planed first as far as the square part, and the slope finished afterwards.

It is also necessary to cut the dovetail housings to receive the fixed shelf. Note from Fig. 3 that this tapers towards the front, this simplifying the fitting in that the joint is loose until it is nearly home.

The inner surfaces should be cleaned up ; also the front rebate. Lastly, the mitres are sawn, and the whole is then assembled. The glue having set the joints are levelled, and the outer surfaces finally cleaned up.

Stand. Fig. 3 shows how this is made. Both legs and rails are prepared square, and the shaping done afterwards. Haunched

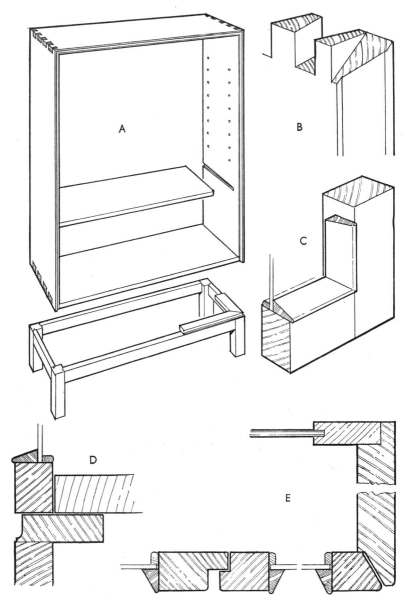

FIG. 3.   A. CARCASE AND STAND CONSTRUCTION.   B. TOP DOVETAILS.   C. DOOR DETAIL.   D. ENLARGED BOTTOM SECTION.   E. PLAN SECTION.

tenons are used. Put the two ends together independently, and add front and back rails when the glue has set. After levelling the top surfaces the moulding is mitred round. The side mouldings run right through at the back, and a plain piece is butted between them along the back rail.

Back. This can be either a single panel of ply; or it can be panelled; or be of the muntin type. In the latter case the muntins are notched over top and bottom so that the panels can be fixed on flush.

Doors. Fig. 1 shows the rather attractive effect obtained by using squared edge stuff and adding the simple chamfered mouldings all round (see (E), Fig. 3). There are three cross bars to each door, those immediately above the wood panels being $\frac{1}{2}$ in. thick, and the two top ones $\frac{1}{4}$ in. They are sub-tenoned in. Simple tenons with haunches are used for the main framing. Note from (E), Fig. 3 that the inner stile of the left-hand door is extra wide to enable a rebated joint to be made. One other point to keep in mind is that the doors have to be bevelled so that they fit into the sloping rebates at top and sides.

After gluing up and fitting, the mouldings are added. To prepare these, the stuff is prepared to the greatest thickness, and the rounded front worked with a $\frac{1}{8}$-in. bead plane. The surface is then bevelled down to the bead with the ordinary bench plane.

To ensure that the mouldings are set in evenly, a gauge is run round the inner edges including the bars. One or two veneer pins driven in on the gauge mark give a definite position.

Beads are mitred round at the back to hold the glass panes in position. Since the door frames are quite light it is a good plan to make the plywood panels a close fit in the rebates as this resists any tendency for the doors to drop.

Short screws have to be used for hingeing, as otherwise they may penetrate through the fairly thin wood left by the sloping rebate.

To finish use white or transparent polish, followed when hard with wax.

For cutting list see page 195.

DWARF BOOKSHELVES

The joints form a decorative feature of the bookcase, no attempt being made to conceal them. As the ends taper from 8 in. at the bottom to 6 in. at the top, it is necessary to work from the back edges. Plane both to the finished size and mark the shelf positions on both sides. The ends are lightly grooved as well as mortised, this preventing any possibility of movement. The grooves are stopped near the front and the shelves shouldered. The shelves stand in at the back by the thickness of the back, the ends being rebated by this amount. When the mortises are cut they should be about $\frac{1}{16}$ in. fuller at each side at the outside to allow for the wedges. Normally wedges are inserted at right angles with the grain, but the wood is sufficiently wide to be free from any liability to split.

Through-dovetail the top and bottom to the ends. A point to note is that a mitre must be allowed at the back (top) so that the rebate can be taken right through as at D.

Assemble the whole thing dry and level the front edges where necessary. Separate the parts and work the small square along top edges of top, bottom, and shelves, and outer edges of ends. Glue up, driving in wedges to close the joints outside without forcing them.

Clean up the whole thing when the glue has set and finish the small square at the top where it runs across the ends. Finally, make the feet, screwing them upwards from beneath.

CUTTING LIST

	Long ft. in.	Wide in.	Thick in.		Long ft. in.	Wide in.	Thick in.
2 Ends	3 0	8¼	¾	1 Bottom ..	2 3¼	8	¾
1 Top	2 3¼	6¼	¾				ply
1 Shelf	2 3¼	6¼	¾	1 Back	3 0	27	¼
1 ,, ...	2 3¼	7¼	¾	2 Feet	10¼	2¼	1¼
1 ,, ...	2 3¼	7¾	¾				

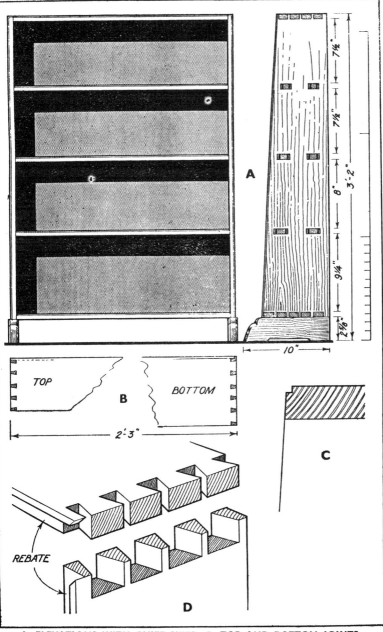

A. ELEVATIONS WITH CHIEF SIZES. B. TOP AND BOTTOM JOINTS.
C. SECTION THROUGH TOP. D. CLOSE-UP VIEW OF TOP JOINT FROM REAR.

TEA TROLLEY

A feature of this trolley is that the top is in the form of a loose tray, enabling it to be lifted off for loading or serving. A drawer which can be pulled out from either end is fitted beneath the top, and there is a commodious shelf below for extra items. Exact overall sizes are not important, but those given are suitable for the small house.

Framework. Prepare the legs to finish $1\frac{1}{4}$ or $1\frac{3}{8}$ in. square and mark out the joints, cramping all four together so that the marks can be squared across all. Lower end rails and top side rails are tenoned in, but the end top rails should be dovetailed as in Fig. 4. Corresponding rails have the shoulders squared across both at the same time to ensure their being alike. Although tenons are usually

FIG. I. TROLLEY WITH LOOSE TRAY TOP.

haunched it is advisable to omit them on the side rails as the leg is already cut away considerably by the dovetails.

Having cut and fitted the joints the rebates are worked in the top rails, the parts cleaned up, and the corners lightly rounded over. Put the ends together first and add the side rails after the glue has

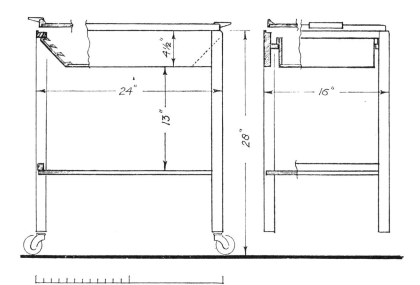

FIG. 2. ELEVATIONS IN PART SECTION WITH MAIN SIZES.

set. It will be realised that the side rails are made extra deep, partly to mask the drawer, and also to give rigidity since there are no lower side rails. Test for squareness and freedom from winding in both elevation and plan. It is necessary to continue the rebates into the legs at the top ; also the rounding-over of the edges.

Shelf. The shelf, of ⅜-in. plywood, is screwed beneath the side rails and looks neater if the edges are lipped with solid wood and lightly rounded. It is polished before being finally fixed. Detail of the tray is given in Fig. 3. A rebated and chamfered edging is mitred round and the ⅜-in. plywood panel screwed in. It is not fixed finally until after the panel and edging have been polished. Handles are fitted as shown, the edging being cut away locally and screws driven in from beneath.

Drawer construction is the last job. Both ends slope, the sides being lap-dovetailed as shown. Rebates at the bottom edge enable the bottom to be fixed, the sides finishing level with the rebate. The latter is made extra deep so that the slight projection provides a grip for the fingers when opening. Screws are used to fix the bottom. The drawer is slung on projecting runners screwed to the side rails, these engaging with strips glued and screwed to the top edges of the drawer sides as shown in the end elevation in Fig. 2.

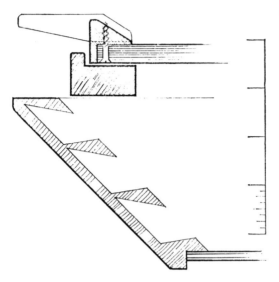

FIG. 3. SECTION
THROUGH TRAY END,
AND DRAWER DETAIL.

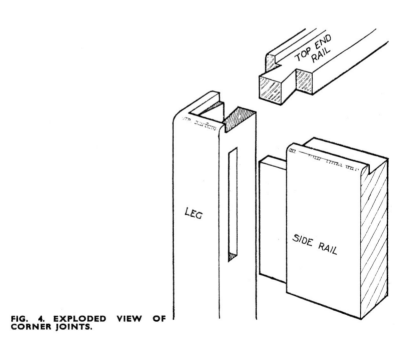

TOP END RAIL

LEG

SIDE RAIL

FIG. 4. EXPLODED VIEW OF
CORNER JOINTS.

A job of this kind is best finished with either table-top polish or with one of the catalyst finishes. The former is rubber applied, whereas the brush is generally used for the other.

CUTTING LIST

	Long ft.	Wide in.	Thick in.	in.		Long ft.	Wide in.	Thick in.	in.
4 Legs	2	2	—	1¼ sq.	2 Edgings ..	1	4	1	⅞
2 Side rails ..	2	0	4¾	⅞	2 Drawer fronts	1	1	5½	⅞
2 End rails ..	1	4	1½	⅞	2 ,, sides..	2	0	3¾	⅜
2 ,, ,, ..	1	4	—	⅞ sq.	1 ,, bottom	1	4½	13	3/16
1 Shelf	2	0	16	⅜ ply	2 Runners ..	2	0	1¼	⅞
1 Tray	2	0	16	⅜ ply	2 Strips ..	2	0	⅞	⅜
2 Edgings ..	2	0	1	⅞					

Small parts extra.

Working allowance has been made in lengths and widths. Thicknesses are net.

LIGHT STOOL

An item of this kind is useful chiefly as a dressing-table stool. The top can be either in solid strips of light and dark wood as in Fig. 1, or it can consist of a frame covered with plywood with foam rubber on top. Alternatively the rubber can rest upon canvas.

Framework. It is strongly advisable to set this out in full size in front elevation. This enables the slope of the legs and angle of shoulders to be ascertained. The stretcher can be tenoned into the lower end rails or slot-dovetailed from beneath if preferred. Note that there are two cross-rails at the top, these being set down so that they finish flush with the curve as shown in Fig. 3. The tenons can be taken right through and wedged. In addition to the mortises three slots are cut at the inside of each rail to give a fixing to the buttons which hold the top.

FIG. 1.   IDEAL AS DRESSING-TABLE STOOL.

Having cut all joints the curved shape of the top rails can be marked. The simplest way of marking is to spring a lath to a curve and run the pencil around this. The curvature drops $\frac{3}{4}$ in. so that the rail is $1\frac{1}{4}$ in. wide at the middle. Clean up all surfaces that cannot be reached later and assemble. The simplest way is to glue up the top portion as a unit. Test for squareness and freedom from winding and knock in the wedges. The end stretcher rails can also be glued to their pairs of legs. When set the legs can be glued to the top rails and the stretcher rail added to the end rails. A certain amount of straining is necessary.

Top. If a solid top is proposed the eight pieces can be prepared as parallel strips. They have to be at a slight angle to enable the curve to be formed, and the simplest way is to use the rails of the frame as a cradle for assembling.

When finished glue rub the joints, and plane to a sweet curve. For the hollow side an old, worn plane can be used. Note that at the underside tapered bevels are worked at the edges around the curve so that the top appears to be only about $\frac{3}{16}$ in. thick at the ends.

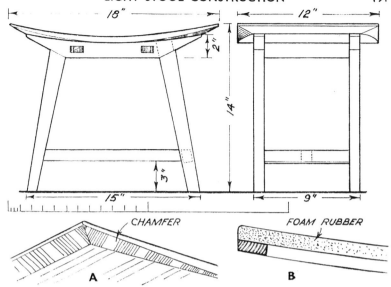

CHAMFER

FOAM RUBBER

A

B

FIG. 2. (above) ELEVA-
TIONS OF STOOL
WITH MAIN SIZES,
AND ALTERNATIVE
SEAT CONSTRUC-
TION.

FIG. 3. (right) HOW
STOOL IS MADE.

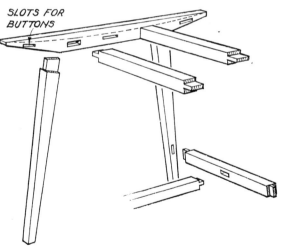

SLOTS FOR
BUTTONS

LIGHT STOOL
CUTTING LIST

	Long ft. in.	Wide in.	Thick in.		Long ft. in.	Wide in.	Thick in.
8 Top pieces ..	1 0½	2½	½	2 Rails	9½	1¾	⅞
4 Legs	1 1½	1¾	⅞	2 Stretcher rails..	9	1½	⅞
2 Rails	1 3½	2¼	⅞	1 Stretcher rail ..	1 2	1¼	⅞

ROOM DIVIDER

An item of this kind can be used either as a room divider, or as a wall cabinet. For the latter the uprights are fixed farther back so that the top section is either level with that below, or stands back about an inch to allow for the skirting. The whole is in three parts; top portion, lower carcase, and stand.

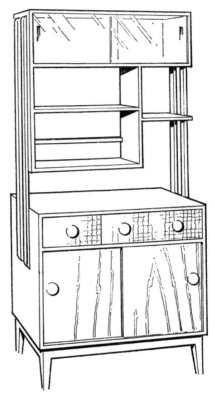

FIG. I.   ATTRACTIVE ITEM WHICH CAN EITHER STAND AGAINST A WALL OR ACT AS A ROOM DIVIDER.

Lower Carcase. This is made as in Fig. 3. In the best way the top corners are mitre-dovetailed, or as a simpler alternative they can double-lap-dovetailed. Bottom is lap-dovetailed, and the drawer rail is stub-tenoned to the ends. An upright drawer division is needed, but, as this is cloaked by the drawer part, it is set back by the front thickness. For the sliding doors grooves must be worked

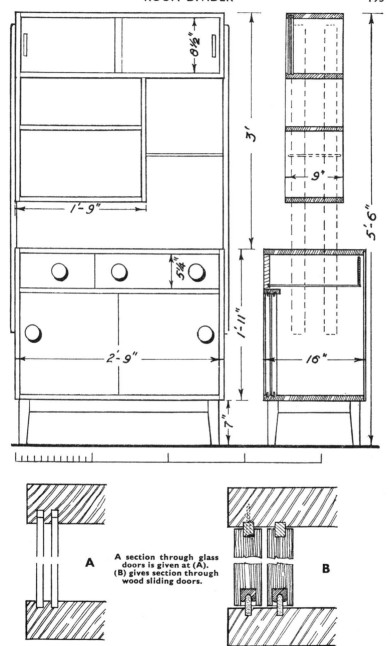

A section through glass doors is given at (A). (B) gives section through wood sliding doors.

FIG. 2. ELEVATIONS WITH SCALE AND MAIN SIZES.

in the bottom to receive fibre track as in Fig. 2. Fibre tracks are unnecessary at the top, plain $\frac{1}{4}$-in. beads being used as shown. The back fits in rebates in top and ends, but is fixed directly to the bottom. Shallow grooves are needed to receive drawer runners.

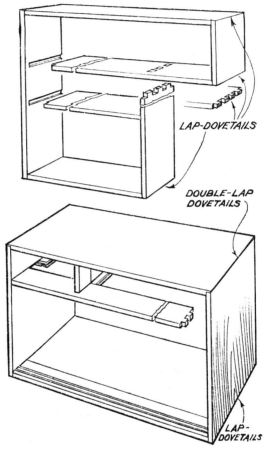

FIG. 3. METHOD OF MAKING THE DIVIDER.

One drawer can be made in normal fashion, but the other must be slot-dovetailed so that the front projects beyond the side and masks the upright. Doors are best made in blockboard or multi-ply with the edges lipped and both sides veneered. At the top grooves are worked to engage with the beads, but at the bottom the grooves are needed to take the gliders. The fibre track itself is narrow but there must be clearance for the gliders. A simple way of arranging for adding doors later is to have the top beads in two lengths joined by a spliced joint. One part can be screwed in position, the door passed in and slid along, and the remaining piece added.

Stand. This is a simple construction with mortise-and-tenon joints. The legs taper at the inside only, and to save having skew shoulders the portion opposite the mortise can be left square.

Upper Portion. Fig. 3 shows how this is made. Plain lap-dovetails can be used at top and bottom since they are not normally seen. The lower inner end should be pinned as shown and wedged from the top because it has to withstand considerable strain. Grooves for the plate glass doors are necessary, those at the top being double the depth of those below so that the doors can be raised up and dropped into the bottom grooves.

Screws driven through from inside are used to hold the end battens, but to give exact position the last named should be cut back about $\frac{1}{16}$ in. or $\frac{1}{8}$ in.

CUTTING LIST

Upper portion		Long ft.	Wide in.	Thick in.			Long ft.	Wide in.	Thick in.
2 Top and shelf		2	9¼	9¼	¾	1 Drawer front	1	0½	5½	¾
2 Bottom and shelf	1	9¼	9¼	¾	1 ,, ,,	1	8	5½	¾
1 End	2	5½	9¼	¾	4 ,, sides	1	3½	5¼	⅜
1 ,, ...	1	8	9¼	¾	1 ,, back	1	0½	5	⅜
1 ,, ...		10¼	9¼	¾	1 ,, ,,	1	7	5	⅜
1 Back ..	2	9	10¼	4	1 ., bottom	1	0	15¼	4
				(mm.)	(ply)				(mm.) (ply)
Lower Carcase						1 ,, ,,	1	7	15¼	4
2 Ends	1	11½	16½	¾					(mm.)
1 Top	2	9¼	16¼	¼					(ply)
1 Bottom ..	2	9	16	¾	**Stand**				
1 Back	2	9	23	⅜	4 Legs		8	—	1¾
				(ply)					(sq.)
1 Rail	2	9	3	¾	2 Rails	2	7½	2	⅞
1 Upright ..		7	3	¾	2 ,, ...	1	3	2	⅞

BOOKCASE (*see page* 180)
CUTTING LIST

		Long ft.	Wide in.	Thick in.			Long ft.	Wide in.	Thick in.
2 Ends		3	10	12⅛	⅞	2 Bars	1	8½	1	¼
1 Top		3	6½	12⅛	⅞	2 Panels ..	1	1	18¾	¼
1 Bottom ..		3	6½	11⅛	⅞	About 42 ft. moulding, ⅝ in. by ⅜ in.,
3 Muntins ..		3	10	1⅝	½	in suitable lengths.
2 Panels ..		3	10	19½	¼	About 42 ft. beading.
1 Fixed Shelf ..		3	5¾	11¼	¾	4 Legs		8½	—	2 sq.
2 Loose shelves		3	4¾	11¼	¾	2 Rails	3	6	2¼	⅞
3 Stiles		3	11	1⅞	⅞	2 ,, ...	1	0	2¼	⅞
1 Stile		3	11	2	⅞	1 Moulding ..	3	6	2	⅝
4 Rails		1	8½	1¾	⅞	1 ,, ..	3	4	2	⅝
4 Bars		1	8½	1	¼	2 ,, ..	1	0½	2	⅝

C.M.F.B.—14

EXTENDING DINING TABLE

A closed size of 45 in. by 36 in., opening to just over 57 in. by 36 in., is convenient for the average dining-room. Those who prefer could reduce the width to 33 in. There are two sliding tops which pull out to enable a loose leaf to be dropped in.

In the table in Fig. 1 the tops are made from $\frac{3}{4}$-in. gaboon multiply veneered with mahogany on both sides. An edging of oak is mitred round and tongued.

Framework. This consists of $\frac{7}{8}$-in. rails tenoned into turned legs which finish $2\frac{1}{4}$ in. at the top. There are no squares on the legs, the rails being taken directly into the round. The simplest way of

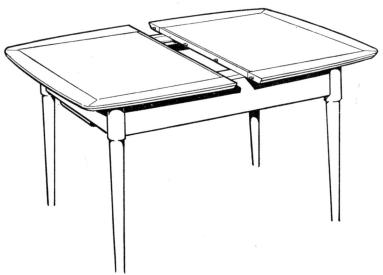

FIG. I. USEFUL SIZE OF TABLE GIVING EXTENSION FROM 45 in. BY 36 in. UP TO 57 in. BY 36 in.

arranging the joint is to cut flats on the legs opposite the joints as in Fig. 3. Those who have a mortiser can do this accurately by fitting a rotary miller bit. Those who have to work entirely by hand will have to set out the flats accurately as shown in Fig. 5. A V-shaped block to hold the rounded leg is prepared. Its width is the same as the diameter of the leg. One diameter at the end can be marked by squaring up from the bottom, and the other by using the gauge again from the bottom. To mark the lines or the flats, and afterwards the mortise lines, the mortise gauge can be used.

Put two ends of the table together independently and allow the glue to set before adding the remaining rails. The lower outer edges of the rails are radiused.

Bearers and slides. Rebated bearers are fixed to the framework sides, and corresponding slides beneath the tops. Often square rebates are cut half-way in both, but it makes a stronger job if they are sloped as in Fig. 4. Lapped dovetails are used to fix the bearers to the end rails, the dovetails being positioned so that they clear the rebates (see Fig. 3). Counter-bored screws are used along the length, and it is necessary to bore the holes before the rebates are worked (see Fig. 4).

Put the dovetails in dry and mark inside the rails the line of the sloping rebate. Square down a line giving the width of the slide, and mark in the thickness with the gauge. Remove the waste by sawing across the grain and chopping away with the chisel. Clearly the sloping cut must align with that of the bearer. When nearly down to the line put in the bearer, gluing right along the edge and screwing. Any unevenness can be levelled afterwards.

Since the slides are of the same section as the bearers they can be prepared at the same time. Each is fitted individually in its notch and numbered.

Tops. The veneering is by the caul or hammer method—unless a press is available. Front and back should be veneered simultaneously, and assuming cauls to be used, it is necessary to use several pairs of cross-bearers slightly bowed in length so that pressure is applied at the centre first, driving the glue out at the edges. Scotch glue is advisable.

The glue having set the edges should be trimmed square all round. To work the tongue grooves the most convenient method is to use the portable router with a deep fence attached so that it can be held upright without difficulty. Theoretically, the edgings are grooved with the same setting as the plywood, but in practice it is advisable to alter it slightly so that the lipping stands up a trifle proud. This enables it to be levelled afterwards.

The edging is mitred round three sides of each main top, and a $\frac{1}{2}$-in. lipping screwed on at the closing edges. In the case of the leaf only the short ends have a wide lipping. Note that the tongue groove is continued a short way along each mitre.

To level the surface a finely set smoothing plane is essential. The scraper follows, and finally glasspaper, Middle 2, $1\frac{1}{2}$, and flour.

Movement of tops. To ensure that the slides are parallel the tops are laid face down on the floor, and the framework placed in the exact position. The slides, which should be free from undue

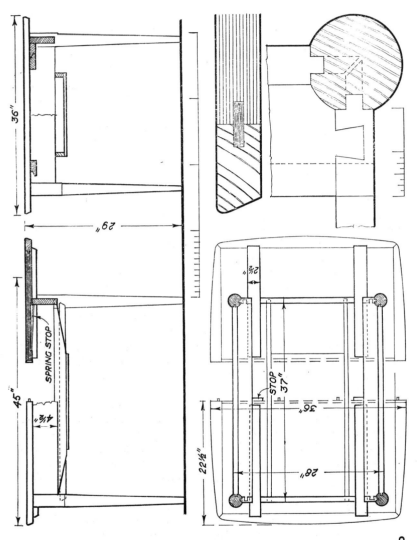

FIG. 2. ELEVA-
TIONS, PLAN, AND
ENLARGED DE-
TAIL.

friction without being slack, are placed over the tops, held close up to the bearers, and fixed with two screws each. The remaining screws are added after testing for correct running. A gap of about $1\frac{1}{4}$ in. is left between the ends of the slides, and stops are later screwed beneath the bearers as in Fig. 3. These stops ensure that the tops are about central when closed.

To prevent the tops from being pulled right out spring stops are let in beneath as in Fig. 6. Recesses to take them are cut in the tops, and one end sloped slightly so that the piece of $\frac{1}{8}$-in. hardwood which forms the spring stands up about $\frac{1}{8}$ in. It hits against the end rail when the top is pulled out. By pressing it in, however, the top can be slid right out when required. Both main tops and leaf have four dowels let in thus ensuring exact registration.

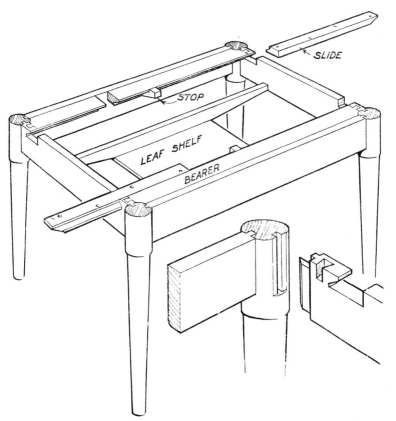

FIG. 3. TOPS REMOVED SHOWING SLIDING ACTION.

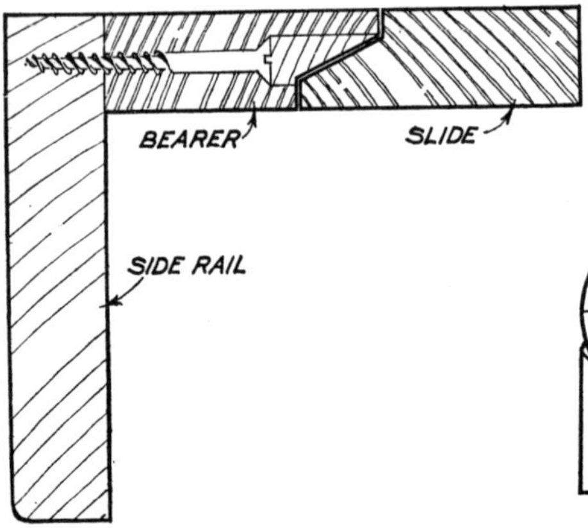

FIG. 4. SECTION THROUGH RAIL SHOWING BEARERS AND SLIDES.

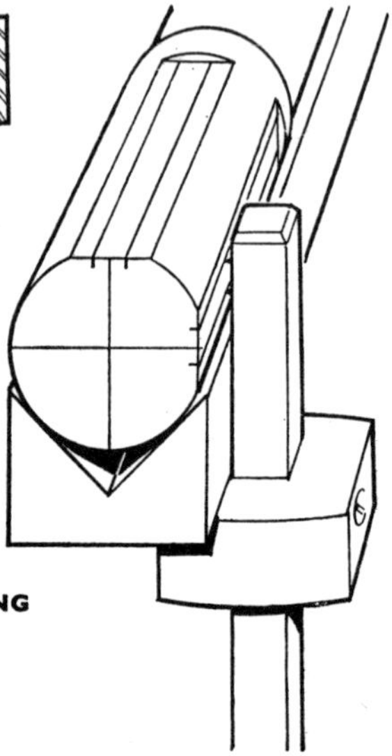

FIG. 5 (*above*). HOW LEG MORTISES CAN BE MARKED.

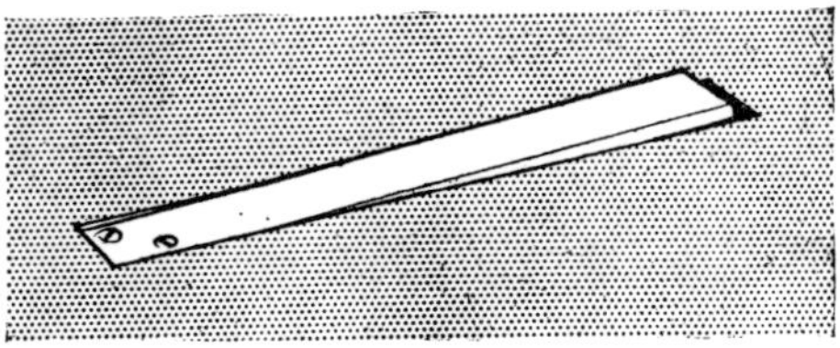

FIG. 6 (*left*). SPRING STOPS FOR SLIDING LEAVES.

Leaf shelf. This is a piece of plywood screwed between two stretchers as in Fig. 3. Notches are cut in the end rails to take the stretchers which are screwed up. There should be about $\frac{1}{4}$ in. clearance beneath the rails for the leaf.

CUTTING LIST

	Long		Wide	Thick		Long		Wide	Thick
	ft.	in.	in.	in.		ft.	in.	in.	in.
4 Legs	2	6	$2\frac{1}{2}$ sq.	—	2 Tops	2	$8\frac{1}{4}$	$20\frac{1}{4}$	$\frac{3}{4}$
2 Rails	3	1	$4\frac{3}{4}$	$\frac{7}{8}$	1 Leaf	2	$8\frac{1}{4}$	$12\frac{1}{4}$	$\frac{3}{4}$
2 ,, ...	2	4	$4\frac{3}{4}$	$\frac{7}{8}$	2 Edgings ..	3	$0\frac{1}{2}$	$2\frac{1}{4}$	$\frac{7}{8}$
2 Bearers ..	3	1	$2\frac{3}{4}$	$\frac{7}{8}$	4 ,, ..	1	11	$2\frac{1}{4}$	$\frac{7}{8}$
4 Slides ..	1	$8\frac{1}{2}$	$2\frac{3}{4}$	$\frac{7}{8}$	2 ,, ..	1	$1\frac{1}{2}$	$2\frac{1}{4}$	$\frac{7}{8}$
2 Stretchers ..	3	1	$2\frac{1}{2}$	$\frac{7}{8}$	4 ,, ..	2	9	$\frac{7}{8}$	$\frac{1}{2}$
1 Shelf	1	6	$15\frac{1}{4}$	$\frac{1}{4}$					

Small parts extra.

LONG COFFEE TABLE

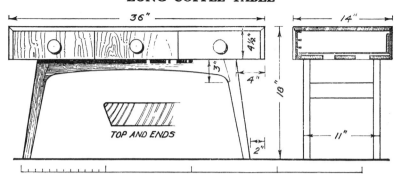

FIG. I.   FRONT AND SIDE ELEVATIONS WITH SCALE.

The carcase is made as in Fig. 2.   Note that the lower drawer rail
and uprights stand in by the thickness of the drawer fronts plus
the bevel as shown in Fig. 1.   At the back and centre are corresponding rails.   The gaps between the rails are filled in with short pieces,
the grain running in the same direction.   Alternatively a solid
bottom could be used, this being lap-dovetailed in.   Drawers are as
at (D), Fig. 2.   Those at the ends have normal dovetails, but the
centre one is slip-dovetailed since the sides have to stand in so that
the front masks the uprights.

Stand construction is as at (B) Fig. 2.

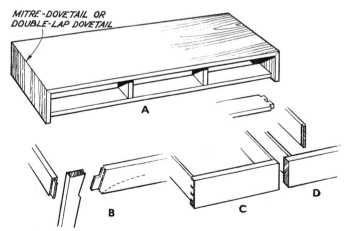

FIG. 2.   CONSTRUCTION DETAILS.

LONG COFFEE TABLE—CUTTING LIST.

		Long ft.	in.	Wide in.	Thick in.
1	Top	3	0½	14½	⅝
2	Ends		5	14½	⅝
3	Rails	3	0	3¼	⅝
2	Uprights ..		4½	3¼	⅝
1	Back	3	0	4½	4 mm. ply

		Long ft.	in.	Wide in.	Thick in.
3	Drawer fronts	1	0	4¼	¾
6	,, sides	1	1½	3¾	⅜
2	,, backs	1	0	3¼	⅜

			Long ft.	in.	Wide in.	Thick in.
1	Drawer	back		11	3¼	⅜
2	,,	bottoms		11½	13	4 mm. ply
1	,,	,,		11	13	4 mm. ply

			Long ft.	in.	Wide in.	Thick in.
4	Legs ..	..	1	3	2	1
2	Rails ..	..	2	4¼	3¼	1
2	,, ..	..		11	2½	1

INDEX